Prayers for Healing

David Adam
Rupert Bristow
Nick Fawcett
Susan Sayers
Ray Simpson

MINNEAPOLIS

Prayers compiled from:

1,000 Prayers for Public Worship — David Adam
Prayers for Inclusion and Diversity — Rupert Bristow
2,000 Prayers for Public Worship — Nick Fawcett
Selected Prayers for Public Worship — Nick Fawcett
More Short Prayers for Public Worship — Nick Fawcett
Prayers for All Seasons — Nick Fawcett
Prayers for All Seasons 2 — Nick Fawcett
1,500 Prayers for Public Worship — Susan Sayers
His Complete Celtic Prayers — Ray Simpson

Augsburg Books
MINNEAPOLIS

PRAYERS FOR HEALING

Copyright © 2013 David Adam, Rupert Bristow, Nick Fawcett, Susan Sayers, and Ray Simpson
Original edition published in English under the title PRAYERS FOR HEALING by Kevin Mayhew Ltd, Buxhall, England.
This edition copyright © Fortress Press 2019

All rights reserved. Except for brief quotations in critical articles or reviews, no part of this book may be reproduced in any manner without prior written permission from the publisher. Email copyright@augsburgfortress.org or write to Permissions, Fortress Press, PO Box 1209, Minneapolis, MN 55440-1209.

Cover image: Cover photo by RobertAx from iStock
Cover design: Tory Herman

Print ISBN: 978-1-5064-5945-5

About the Authors

DAVID ADAM was the Vicar of Lindisfarne, off the Northumbrian coast, for thirteen years until he retired in March 2003. His work involved ministering to thousands of pilgrims and other visitors. He is the author of many inspiring books on spirituality and prayer, and his Celtic writings have rekindled a keen interest in our Christian heritage.

RUPERT BRISTOW was Director of Education for Canterbury Diocese and a governor of Canterbury Christ Church University from 1995 until his retirement in 2008 and is active as a Reader in Trinity Benefice, Folkestone. He has worked in education—in schools, universities, and administrations—at home and overseas. He has also been a specialist adviser to a House of Commons select committee, edited and written for various educational publications, and chaired Kent SACRE (Standing Advisory Council for Religious Education). He is an Honorary Fellow of Canterbury Christ Church University.

NICK FAWCETT was brought up in Southend-on-Sea, Essex, and trained for the Baptist ministry at Bristol and Oxford, before serving churches in Lancashire and Cheltenham. He subsequently spent three years as a chaplain with the Christian movement Toc H, before focusing on writing and editing, which he continues with today, despite wrestling with cancer. He lives with his wife, Deborah, and two children—Samuel and Kate—in Wellington, Somerset, worshipping at the local Anglican church. An enthusiastic walker, he delights in the beauty of the Somerset and Devon countryside around his home, his numerous books owing much to the inspiration he unfailingly finds there.

SUSAN SAYERS is the author of many popular resource books for the church. Through the conferences and workshops she is invited to lead, she has been privileged to share in the worship of many different traditions and cultures. A teacher by profession, she was ordained a priest in the Anglican Church and, before her retirement, her work was divided between the parish of Westcliff-on-Sea, the local women's prison, writing, training days, and retreats.

RAY SIMPSON is a Celtic new monastic for tomorrow's world, a lecturer, consultant, liturgist, and author of some 30 books. He is the founding guardian of the international Community of Aidan and Hilda and the pioneer of its e-studies programs. He is an ordained member of the Christian church and lives on the Holy Island of Lindisfarne. His website is www.raysimpson.org.

1   Come, Lord, to our weakness
    and fill us with your power.
    Come to our weariness and renew us.
    Come to our troubles with your peace.
    Come, Lord, change us and we shall be changed.
    David Adam

2   We rejoice in your abiding presence
    and pray for all who feel lonely or anxious at this time.
    We remember all who are fearful of the future
    and those who are terminally ill.
    We pray for those who await a doctor's diagnosis
    or who are preparing to go into the hospital.
    We ask your blessing upon all who suffer
    and upon those who care for them.   *David Adam*

3   We pray for all who are fearful for their future,
    those who are awaiting a doctor's diagnosis
    or an operation,
    or all who are terminally ill.
    Lord, bless all who work in caring for others
    and relieving their anxiety.   *David Adam*

4   God of love and peace, we remember before you
    all who are weighed down with anxiety or fear.
    We pray for those who are depressed
    and those who feel they can no longer cope with life.
    We ask your blessing upon all who are ill
    and all who suffer in any way.
    May they come to know your love and your peace.
    David Adam

5   Lord, we remember all disturbed and distressed people,
    all who have suffered from traumatic events
    or who are troubled in spirit.
    We pray for all who are exhausted or depressed
    at this time,
    for all who can find no rest.   *David Adam*

6 Lord, we ask your blessing
upon all who are discouraged or despondent
at this time,
upon all who feel that life is not worthwhile.
May they know of your love and your presence.
David Adam

7 Lord of life, we remember all who are dispirited,
the distressed, the depressed, and despairing,
all who have lost hope or joy in their lives.
We pray for all who fear the future,
all who have lost sight of you and your love.
We remember also all who are struggling
with poverty or hunger,
the homeless and the refugee. *David Adam*

8 We pray today for all who are anxious and overworked,
all who are world-weary or deeply troubled.
We remember especially
any who feel the lack of love or attention;
those who feel neglected or unwanted.
We ask your blessing upon all who are ill
and those who have been taken into care. *David Adam*

9 We seek your blessing
upon all who are oppressed or depressed,
upon all whose lives are filled with sorrow or pain.
We remember those who are battling
with a long-term illness
and those who feel they are losing mobility or agility.
We remember in your presence
all who are struggling at this time. *David Adam*

10 Father, we pray for all who have lost their way in life.
We remember those who have lost faith
in themselves, in others, or in their God.
We pray for all who are finding life desperate
and are disillusioned or fearful.

We ask you to comfort and bless
all who are struggling
with illness or problems that they cannot solve
and those who feel unable to find help or hope.
David Adam

11 We give thanks for our peace of mind
and we pray for all who are disturbed or distressed.
We remember those who have had a traumatic experience
and those who have suffered from betrayal or violence.
We pray for all who are not at peace
with themselves or with others. *David Adam*

12 We pray for all who are struggling with life,
those who are burdened with guilt or anger,
all who have memories that disturb them. *David Adam*

13 Lord, we bring before you all whose lives are fragmented;
people who are broken in body, mind, or spirit.
We remember all who feel shattered and exhausted,
all who long for your healing touch.
We pray for all who seek hope and peace,
that they may come to you and rest in your presence.
David Adam

14 You are our hope and strength, O Lord.
We come to you for refreshment and renewal.
When we are weak, may we trust in your strength.
When we are fearful, may we turn to you and your light.
We pray for all who are struggling at this time.
We remember before you the troubled in mind
and the distressed in spirit. *David Adam*

15 We give thanks for the renewing powers of our bodies
and for all who share in the healing and care of others.
We pray for all who feel their lives are empty
or meaningless,
all who feel they have wasted their lives
or never fully lived. *David Adam*

16   Lord, we remember all who are struggling
with doubt, depression, and despair,
all who are having difficulty in their daily lives.
We pray for all who are ill at home or in the hospital,
especially those who have no one
to care for them or visit them. *David Adam*

17   Lord, we remember before you
the troubled in mind,
all who have painful memories,
the depressed and the despairing,
the mentally disturbed,
and all who cannot cope with life.
Lord, keep our minds strong
in the knowledge and love of God
and help us to proclaim your presence and love. *David Adam*

18   We ask you to bless
all who are not at peace with themselves,
all who are disturbed in mind or spirit.
We ask that all who are ill at this time
may know your love and your presence. *David Adam*

19   We remember all who walk in darkness
and who are heavily burdened.
We pray for all who have lost hope and who despair.
We ask your blessing
upon all who are chronically ill
and those who can no longer cope on their own.
We pray for all who are approaching death and
their loved ones who are caring for them. *David Adam*

20   Lord, we pray for your blessing
upon the world-weary, the worried, and worn,
all who feel overwhelmed and unable to cope.
We remember all who are ill at home or in the hospital
and those who care for them.
We pray especially for any involved in accidents
or whose illness finds no cure. *David Adam*

21   We remember all who feel weary with life,
      drained of energy, and no longer able to cope.
      We pray for all who struggle against great odds.
      We ask your blessing upon all who feel alone
      and that no one cares for them.   *David Adam*

22   Lord God,
      when the days are dark and we are weary,
      when the stress and the storms increase
      and we are in danger of being overwhelmed,
      hear us and help us.
      May we know you are always with us
      and ready to help us.   *David Adam*

23   We remember before you
      all who feel confused or troubled at this time.
      We pray for all who are distressed
      and those who are not able to cope
      with what is happening around them.
      May they know your presence and your power.
      We ask your blessing upon all who are ill
      at home or in the hospital,
      especially those who are fearful or lonely.   *David Adam*

24   May we not lose sight of things eternal
      among all that happens in our lives.
      We ask your blessing upon all who find life dull,
      all who are depressed or have lost hope.
      We pray for all who struggle with illness
      or difficult circumstances.   *David Adam*

25   We give thanks that you are our strength and salvation.
      We remember all who are broken by illness.
      We pray for those struggling with a nervous breakdown
      and all who feel their lives are on the edge of collapse.
      We ask your blessing upon all
      who are no longer able to care for themselves.   *David Adam*

26   We remember all who are suffering from mental stress,
all who are experiencing a breakdown
of their lives or their personalities.
We pray for those taken into care
and those who are a danger to themselves or others.
We ask your blessing upon those
who are suffering from mental anguish or trauma.
We pray for all who are seeking to restore
health and peace to individuals or communities.
David Adam

27   We remember before you
all who are suffering alone with no one to help.
We pray for those who are in isolation wards
and all who are unable
to join in the full life of the community.
We remember also those we know
who are in the hospital at this time.   *David Adam*

28   We give thanks for the gifts of hearing and speech.
We remember all who suffer from deafness
and those who are unable to speak.
We pray for all who suffer from autism,
all who are withdrawn from normal life,
and all who find communication difficult.   *David Adam*

29   We pray for all who are ill at home or in the hospital.
We remember families where the mother is ill
or where she is tending an ill child.
We ask your blessing upon families
where there is poverty or the inability to cope.   *David Adam*

30   We remember all exhausted peoples,
the world-weary, the depressed, and the discouraged.
We pray for all who despair
and all who feel they can no longer cope with life.
David Adam

31   We pray for all who suffer from autism
or have problems communicating.
We remember those who suffer from deafness
or the inability to speak.
We pray for those who are suffering
from Alzheimer's disease
and all who are too frail or ill to look after themselves.
David Adam

32   We pray for all who suffer from blindness
or impairment of their sight,
for those who suffer from river blindness.
We ask you to bless
all who seek to relieve their suffering
and to restore sight.
We pray for any who have lost vision
of you and your love.   *David Adam*

33   Holy and strong One, we remember before you
all who suffer from weakness or illness,
all who suffer from being handicapped
or restricted in their lives.
May they know that you love them
and continue to call them.
We ask your blessing on all who are called to work
in hospitals, doctors' offices, and health centers.
We pray for friends and loved ones who are ill. *David Adam*

34   God of love, we remember all
who have been involved in accidents this week.
We pray for all who have been injured
and those who are bereaved.
We pray for those who have gone into the hospital
and all who are ill at home.   *David Adam*

35   God, you are ever-present.
We ask you to strengthen and support
all who are overwhelmed by the storms of life.
We remember those whose sickness finds no cure.
We pray for loved ones and caregivers who feel exhausted
and unable to cope anymore.   *David Adam*

36   We remember all who are strengthened
by their faith and trust in you.
We ask you to bless all whose sickness finds no cure.
We pray for the terminally ill
and all who are in hospice
or need permanent care in a home.
We pray for all who feel their life is wasting away.
David Adam

37   We give thanks that you are a God who heals and restores,
that you care for our whole being—
body, mind, and spirit.
We remember in your presence
all who have been injured in accidents
or through acts of violence,
all who have become ill suddenly
and those whose illness has no cure.
We pray for their well-being
and the knowledge of your love.
Lord, bless all who share in healing.
David Adam

38   We remember all who are isolated through illness.
We pray for those who are in a hospital or in a home
and who have no visitors.
We remember those from our own community
who are ill at home or in the hospital.
David Adam

39   We give thanks for the healing power of faith.
We ask you to bless and guide all who heal.
We remember our own doctor and surgery.
We ask that the ill and the weary may know you
as their companion and helper.
We pray to you for all who are hard-pressed
and struggling.
David Adam

40   Lord, let your presence bring comfort to the suffering;
may they know your love and care.
We remember all who are paralyzed
or suffering from strokes,
all who are unable to move about freely
and all who are homebound.
David Adam

41 We pray for all who have been ill for a long time,
    for those whose illness finds no cure.
    We pray for all
    who feel they are losing their faculties or mobility,
    all who cannot cope on their own.
    We remember those who are in hospice. *David Adam*

42 God, we ask your presence to bring comfort and hope
    to all who are struggling at this time.
    We remember those injured in accidents or acts of violence,
    those who are ill
    and all who are in the hospital. *David Adam*

43 We give thanks that nothing can separate us
    from your love.
    We ask your blessing upon all
    who are ill, lonely, or oppressed.
    We remember friends and loved ones
    who are in the hospital or ill at home
    and all who are caring for them.
    We pray also for all who despair,
    all who have lost hope or any vision of your love.
    David Adam

44 We come with all who are in pain or sorrow.
    We remember those whose sickness finds no cure,
    those who are permanently ill,
    and those with a short time to live. *David Adam*

45 We come before you with all who are struggling:
    those who are ill at home or in the hospital;
    the world's poor, the oppressed,
    and all who suffer from violence or rejection.
    We ask that we may know your healing presence.
    David Adam

46   Loving Lord, we ask your blessing
upon all who are ill at home or in the hospital.
We remember also loved ones
who are caring for them
and are anxious and fearful.
We pray for all who cannot cope on their own.
We ask your blessing upon all caregivers
and those involved in medical treatment
and the rescue services. *David Adam*

47   We remember all who are struggling
with illness or with fear.
We ask your blessing
upon all who are in the hospital,
all who have been injured
through violence or accidents.
We pray for all who are fearful of the future. *David Adam*

48   We give thanks for all who share in healing
and the restoring of well-being to all who suffer.
We remember all who are in pain or distress
at this time.
We ask your blessing
upon all who are separated from loved ones
through illness or disability
and all who can no longer cope on their own. *David Adam*

49   Lord of light, we ask your blessing
upon all who are struggling with darkness and fear.
We remember those who have been involved
in accidents or in acts of violence this week.
We pray for all who have suddenly become ill
and those who are in the hospital.
We pray for all who anxiously await
the results of a medical examination. *David Adam*

50   Loving God, we give thanks
for our health and well-being.
We ask your blessing upon all who are ill
at home or in the hospital.
We remember today all who suffer
from autism or schizophrenia
and all who are mentally ill.
We ask your blessing upon all
who are separated from their loved ones through illness
and all who feel rejected. *David Adam*

51   Lord, transform our darkness with your light.
We ask your blessing
upon all who are struggling with illness
or who are no longer able to cope on their own.
We pray for all who have been injured
in accidents or through violence. *David Adam*

52   Lord, we come to you for renewal and healing,
for strength and for light.
We ask your blessing
upon all who suffer from a disability
or who are ill at this time.
We remember those who are blind, lame, or deaf
and those who suffer from leprosy.
We pray for all who have recently lost loved ones
and for those who are caring for the terminally ill.
David Adam

53   Lord, you are with us even when it is dark.
We ask your blessing upon all who are in pain or in fear.
We pray for those who are ill at home or in the hospital
and all who have been injured this week.
We remember those who feel life has little meaning
and those who have lost their way
or who are anxious about their future. *David Adam*

54 We give thanks for our health and well-being.
We remember in your presence
all who have suddenly become ill
or been injured in accidents,
and those whose lives have been darkened
by the loss of a loved one.
We ask your blessing
upon all who are homeless or hungry
and all who fear the future.
May they know your presence
and so have courage and hope in their troubles.
David Adam

55 We give thanks for the medical profession
and for all who care for our well-being.
We ask your blessing upon all who are ill
at home or in the hospital.
We remember any who have been injured
in accidents or through acts of violence.   *David Adam*

56 Lord, bless all who feel restricted
by what is happening around them.
We remember all who live in violent or deprived areas.
We ask your blessing upon all who are ill
or who have been injured through accidents,
and upon those who care for them.
Lord, give them courage and hope in their troubles.
David Adam

57 We remember all who are ill and suffering at this time,
all who are distressed
and those who are overburdened.
May they know your peace and your presence.
May all who walk in darkness
come to know your light and your love.
We pray for all who are in the hospital
or in care at this time.   *David Adam*

58   We remember before you
     all who are exhausted or world-weary.
     We pray for those who have lost sight
     of where they belong or where they are going.
     We pray for all lonely and marginalized people.
                                                    David Adam

59   We ask your blessing on all who feel lonely,
     all who are neglected,
     and all whose relationships are breaking down.
     We pray for any who have been bereaved
     or who have been deserted by a loved one.   *David Adam*

60   As we rejoice in life, we remember all who feel
     that life is meaningless and empty.
     We ask your blessing on the despairing and despondent.
     We pray for all who are treated as unclean
     through illness or disability.   *David Adam*

61   We remember all who feel unloved and unwanted.
     We pray for homes where there is hatred or violence,
     where there is little respect for each other,
     where there is neglect.
     We ask your blessing upon all
     who have been taken into care.   *David Adam*

62   Lord of love, we remember before you all who are lonely.
     We ask your blessing upon those who are ill or injured.
     We pray for all who are raging against life
     and all who are not at peace with themselves
     or the world.
     We pray for all who have hardened their hearts
     against love.   *David Adam*

63   We remember all who suffer,
     all who are in the hospital,
     all who are lonely and feel rejected,
     all whose lives are in a dark cloud.
     We think of those who are fearful of the future
     and those whose lives are full of sadness.
     Lord, may the light of your love transform their lives.
                                                    David Adam

64 We remember before you all whose voices are unheard,
    people who feel neglected or unwanted.
    We pray for the lonely and those who have no helpers.
    We remember also all who are ill at this time
    at home or in the hospital.   *David Adam*

65 As we rejoice in your presence,
    we remember all who feel lonely
    and neglected in our world.
    We ask your blessing on all who are oppressed
    and those who are struggling to survive.
    We pray for all who are caught up in violence and war,
    and for those not at peace with each other,
    with themselves, and with you.   *David Adam*

66 God, we remember before you
    all who are betrayed in love,
    the broken-hearted and the deserted,
    the rejected and the lonely.
    We thank you for our own loved ones and our friends.
    Lord God, as you love us with an everlasting love,
    help us to love you and show your love
    in our love for each other.   *David Adam*

67 We thank you for the confidence and joy we have
    through knowing we are loved.
    We ask your blessing
    upon all who are lonely or neglected.
    We pray for those separated from their loved ones
    through illness or circumstance.
    We pray for all who have been taken into care.
                                       David Adam

68 We give thanks for the longings that you have given us.
    We ask your blessing upon our loved ones,
    our families, and friends.
    We remember before you all who are lonely,
    those who are failing in health or strength,
    and all who are fearful for the future.   *David Adam*

69 We pray for all who have lost vision and hope,
    for all who are struggling with life.
    We remember the broken-hearted,
    those suffering from broken relationships,
    all who are broken by illness or trouble,
    all who can no longer cope on their own.
    Lord, may they know you in their breaking,
    for you alone can make us whole. *David Adam*

70 We remember all who have lost their way
    and become involved in drugs or violence,
    all who are suffering
    through the decadence of society.
    We ask your blessing
    upon all who are ill at home or in the hospital
    and all who are fearful for their future. *David Adam*

71 We remember today all who are struggling with life.
    We pray for the world's poor, refugees,
    and all who are used as work slaves.
    We ask your blessing upon all who are losing heart
    or who feel discouraged and despondent. *David Adam*

72 Lord, we come with the sorrowful and sad people
    of our world,
    with all who live in fear or anxiety.
    We pray for refugees and homeless people.
    We remember all who are in pain or distress at this time.
    May they all know that you love them and care for them.
    We ask your blessing on all healers
    and on relief organizations. *David Adam*

73 We pray for all who feel they have lost their way,
    who are troubled and distressed,
    that they may know your love and care. *David Adam*

74   Lord, you are always ready to help us in our troubles.
     We bring before you
     the sorrows and sighing of our world.
     We remember all who are ill,
     all injured in accidents or acts of violence,
     all who are hungry or homeless.
     We ask your blessing upon each one
     and on all who care for them.   *David Adam*

75   We come with all who weep by gravesides,
     all who mourn the loss of a loved one,
     all who feel lonely or deserted.
     May all who mourn find new hope and joy in you.
     We remember all who are terminally ill
     and those who are caring for them.
     We think of those who have a heavy weight
     on their hearts and minds
     and tears in their eyes.
     We ask that we may all know the hope of eternal life.
                                                      David Adam

76   Lord God, we ask your blessing
     upon all who feel confused about life
     and all who have lost their way.
     We pray especially for all who are caught up
     in the darkness of despair
     and those involved in drugs or vice.
     We pray for those who live a lie
     and cannot face the truth.
     Lord, bless all who are suffering
     from broken relationships
     and who are troubled in heart.   *David Adam*

77   Come, Lord, to all whose hope is gone,
     the lost, the despairing, and the deeply depressed.
     We remember the overworked, the world-weary,
     the exhausted, and the worn out.

We ask your blessing
upon those who feel wrung out to dry,
all who feel numb,
and those whose senses are deadened.
We pray for all suffering from deep stress or trauma
and their loved ones caring for them. *David Adam*

78 Lord God, we pray today for all who are suffering
from strained or broken relationships.
We remember all who are a bad influence
and lead others astray.
We pray for the lost.
We pray for all caught up in drugs or vice.
May they be given the chance of new directions.
David Adam

79 We remember all who have lost their way
and who feel confused by life,
especially those who feel life has no meaning or purpose.
We pray for all who are captives of vice or drugs.
We ask your blessing
upon all who are fearful,
especially those who are suffering
from persecution or poverty. *David Adam*

80 We pray for areas of our world
where darkness seems to triumph over light.
We remember people who are possessed by drug addiction.
We remember also those
who feel that they are possessed by evil.
May they all come to know the glorious liberty
of the children of God. *David Adam*

81 Lord, we remember before you
all who are suffering through violence or abuse.
We pray especially for those
whose lives are marred by their past or present sins.
We remember also today all who are struggling
with pain or chronic illness
and all who can no longer cope with life on their own.
David Adam

82 Give strength to the weak,
    refresh the weary,
    encourage the fearful,
    and protect all who are endangered.   *David Adam*

83 We pray for all who have lost vision
    or hope in the world,
    all who feel lonely,
    all who have lost a sense of wonder,
    all who have fallen into doubt.   *David Adam*

84 We remember all who are struggling with their faith,
    those who doubt,
    any who sit in darkness, or who live in fear.
    We bring to mind all who have fallen away from the faith,
    especially any known to us.   *David Adam*

85 We give thanks that through Jesus
    we can walk with confidence and hope.
    We ask your blessing upon all who struggle
    in darkness and fear,
    all who feel lost
    and those who are captives to vice and sin.   *David Adam*

86 We give thanks for those who have taught us the faith
    and brought us to know you, O God.
    We remember any who are struggling with their faith
    at this time,
    all who are tempted to despair and to give up.
    We pray especially for all who are sorely troubled
    by circumstances or relationships.   *David Adam*

87 We give thanks for the Church throughout the world;
    for people who are growing in the faith
    and being made strong by their beliefs.
    We remember all who are struggling
    with opposition and evil
    and all whose lives are in danger.
    We remember all who feel oppressed and let down.
    We pray for all whose faith is being challenged
    and those who have lost contact with you. *David Adam*

88   We bring before you all who doubt or despair,
all who are surrounded by darkness or illness.
May they come into the light of your love
and know that you are with them.
We ask you to bless all who have been involved
in accidents or in violence this week.
Give courage and hope to all
who seek to bring your healing and peace.   *David Adam*

89   We remember all whose lives are darkened
by pain and distress;
all who are struggling with doubt and despair;
all whose faith is shaken
by what is happening around them.   *David Adam*

90   As we rejoice in your power,
we remember all whose powers are waning,
the elderly and the infirm
and all who are disabled.
We ask your blessing upon all who are ill
or who have been injured in accidents.
May they find courage and hope in you
and in your abiding love.   *David Adam*

91   We ask your blessing
upon all who are finding life difficult
through illness or oppression.
We pray for all who feel their abilities
are being wasted or thwarted
through illness or circumstance.
May we know
that in whatever circumstance we find ourselves
God still loves us and calls us to love him.   *David Adam*

92 Father, we give thanks for your healing love.
We remember before you all suffering people,
the ill and the hungry,
the world's poor and the unemployed.
We ask your blessing upon all who are terminally ill
and those who are caring for them.
We pray for caregivers who feel exhausted
or who feel they are not appreciated. *David Adam*

93 Lord,
as we enter into the stillness, calm our hearts and our minds.
Let all the storms within us cease, and enfold us in your peace.
We come in weakness to you for strength;
we come in our sinfulness for your forgiveness;
we come wearied by life for your refreshing grace;
we come out of our darkness to your love and light.
Lord, renew, refresh, restore us by your presence
and your power. *David Adam*

94 Risen Lord, we seek your peace:
peace for our war-torn world;
peace between nations and people;
peace in our dealings with each other;
peace in our hearts and homes. *David Adam*

95 We give thanks
for all who work in the healing professions,
and we pray for our own doctors and health workers.
We remember all who are denied healing and help
through poverty or war.
We ask your blessing upon all who are caring
for a loved one who is terminally ill,
and for the work of hospices. *David Adam*

96 Compassionate Lord,
bring us an understanding of your mind,
a glimpse of your truth,
which will help us to know
the extent of your love.

Embrace, we pray, the needs of those
who do not see clearly,
who find it difficult to relate to others,
and who go through phases of illness
in mind, in spirit, in relationship.
Bring calm and healing to troubled minds. *Rupert Bristow*

97   Suffering servant,
make all things new for us,
and especially for those with mental illness.
Make us compassionate through our engagement
and sensitive to the vulnerabilities
of those who are sick.
May we always see the person
behind the behavior,
just as we see you
behind your creation,
knowing what is of you
and what is our contribution,
our value added or taken away. *Rupert Bristow*

98   Lord of health and wholeness,
look down, we pray,
on those who struggle with life.
Set them free from despair
through the glimpse of the hope you bring.
However it seems through the mist of hurt,
let your love dispel the cloud of unknowing
and restore a right relationship
with self, with you, with all around. *Rupert Bristow*

99   God of great expectations,
lift the spirits of all who suffer
from mental strife,
from guilt and pain,
from hate and insecurity.

Open the curtains to our soul
and let the light shine in.
Dispel doubt and fear
from the hearts of those who find it difficult
to face the next day
with the confidence you can inspire. *Rupert Bristow*

100   All-embracing God,
you understand the turmoil of those
whose mental state is a worry to others.
Release the energy of hope
in those who see only danger.
Bring self-knowledge and sensitive care
to the fragile and vulnerable in mind and spirit.
Above all, Lord, create in all of us, we pray,
the capacity to care, the patience to persevere,
as your Son did—and still does. *Rupert Bristow*

101   God of health and wholeness,
we ask for your blessings
on all who are hurting at this time,
through physical pain or mental distress.
May their spirits be raised
by what we do and say.
Most of all, Lord, hold out your healing hand,
and give them the promise
of your comforting presence. *Rupert Bristow*

102   Lord of restoration and recovery,
let us rejoice in physical and mental health,
the joy of being well,
the blessing of staying healthy.
But let us not forget the struggle of illness,
when food, drink, and material things mean little.
May we build up our spiritual resources
so that when illness strikes
we can respond positively to others as to ourselves.
Rupert Bristow

103 Serene Lord,
    may we draw on the serenity of your presence
    when we experience the confusion of our illness.
    May we take heart from the miracles performed by your Son,
    and continued through the disciples.
    And may the modern-day miracles of treatment and care
    go hand in hand with the privilege
    of looking after one another,
    in his steps and to your glory. *Rupert Bristow*

104 Suffering servant, healing Lord,
    let us give thanks that where there is illness,
    there is often a cure, courtesy of your creation;
    and that when a cure is not available,
    you give us other strengths and skills
    to show our love for each other,
    as well as the desire to search,
    search, and search again,
    for the strands and signs
    in your world and in our minds,
    which will unlock the answer. *Rupert Bristow*

105 Immanent God,
    may your presence
    teach us patience,
    bring us transformation,
    point us to the right treatment.
    Help our bodies to help themselves;
    keep us positive, even in suffering;
    and may we always acknowledge
    your presence in our ministry to others. *Rupert Bristow*

106 Sovereign Lord,
    we know that love turned bad
    can lead to horrible things.
    Let our hearts go out to those who have been abused,
    and our powers of forgiveness be tested by those who
    have abused.

We all fall short in our lives.
But let us always call on you,
when feelings of hate or revenge threaten to take over.
Save us from ourselves and bring us back to your true path.

Rupert Bristow

107   Astounding, transforming God,
where you have given us free will
we may stray from the right course.
May we be ever vigilant,
in ourselves and in our dealings with others,
so that evil does not take hold,
damage is not done,
and abuse is confronted.
We pray for victims and perpetrators,
that time and treatment will heal,
with your help, Lord.

Rupert Bristow

108   Maker of heaven and earth,
you have shown us good and warned us of evil.
May we learn the lessons of the past,
in ourselves and over time.
Let us be aware of the signs of abuse,
unafraid of challenging behavior,
but always seeking remedies
for body and soul, heart and mind,
knowing the extent of your reach.

Rupert Bristow

109   God of transformation,
help those traumatized by abuse
be shown the power of true love,
by neighbor, friend, and family,
so that the effects of abuse
can never close the channels to that love,
whatever went before.

Rupert Bristow

110   Loving Lord,
       against all odds may untainted, unconditional love prevail,
       the love your Son showed us,
       the love which restores,
       the love which forgives,
       the love which respects,
       the love which can overcome abuse,
       as long as we can trust you
       and begin to trust each other again.   *Rupert Bristow*

111   Almighty God,
       you have given us the bread of life,
       but also our daily bread.
       You have given us living water,
       as well as water to drink.
       But let us beware the effects of alcohol,
       especially when we drink too much too often.
       If we are addicted, help us to admit it;
       if we seek to recover, make us strong in saying no.
       Bless and preserve our will to be free
       of harm to self or others.   *Rupert Bristow*

112   All-embracing Lord,
       forgive us our frailties and temptations
       as we seek to shed our addictions.
       Let the demon drink be overcome
       as Satan was resisted in the desert.
       But we must remember Satan's
       "what though the field be lost, all is not lost"
       in keeping up the battle against drink, drugs,
       and all that enslaves.   *Rupert Bristow*

113   All-enveloping Lord,
       surround us with hope and trust
       in your steely support
       as we battle to resist addiction,
       in ourselves and in loved ones.

May we be swift to learn
and slow to judge.
Let us be single-minded in our faith
and purposeful in our recovery,
seeking forgiveness for weakness
and showing discipline in rehabilitation. *Rupert Bristow*

114   God of remedy and reconciliation,
help the families of those addicted to drink,
in their sensitive situation.
Give them the patience of Job;
give to addicts Peter's ability to learn from failure;
give to friends a constancy that will be tested;
and let the tentacles of drink
release their grip on lives that
once were lost and now are found again. *Rupert Bristow*

115   Healing Lord,
let nature and the skills of doctors
join forces to mend and tend
all afflicted with cancer.
Let diagnosis be quick and treatment timely,
and may the knowledge of your presence
be a comfort and a shield,
to patient and caregiver alike. *Rupert Bristow*

116   God of the personal,
help us never to make assumptions about people's illness
or the treatment they receive.
May every step of recovery from cancer
be blessed with understanding and thanks,
and every setback be accompanied
by renewed prayer and encouragement.
May we combine the cure of disease with the cure of souls.
Rupert Bristow

117   God of great gifts,
       send me your love;
       show me your concern.
       But moderate our expectations,
       even as we seek your extravagant generosity.
       May we live in hope
       and hold on in faith,
       until the outcome is known
       and your peace takes over.   *Rupert Bristow*

118   God of purpose and promise,
       you take us through the stormy seas of life,
       surfing on waves of joy
       and plunging into depths of despair.
       Be our strong captain
       in navigating us through,
       and may we ride out the weather,
       knowing the calm to come.   *Rupert Bristow*

119   Lord of healing and wholeness,
       we pray for those recovering from cancer
       and those whose treatment is just beginning.
       As each person is different and distinct,
       so each illness is personal and individual.
       May we show our empathy,
       not only in our words and wishes,
       but also in our practical assistance,
       those little unremembered acts
       of kindness, love, and friendship.   *Rupert Bristow*

120   Soothing Lord,
       remember us as we cope with pain
       and strengthen us in our resolve to recover.
       You send us the blessing of life,
       but also the trial of tough times.
       Thank you for the resilience we have
       and the patient friendship of family and friends.
       Give us the grace to accept what we experience
       alongside the hope of deliverance.   *Rupert Bristow*

121   All-seeing God,
        may we give ourselves to your care,
        in partnership with all you have gifted
        with medical, nursing, and care skills.
        May drugs do their work;
        may surgeons display their expertise;
        and may doctors fulfill their duty of care.
        But at the center of everything,
        may we see your bright star,
        to ease our pain and see us home.   *Rupert Bristow*

122   Dear Lord,
        heal us,
        strengthen us,
        prepare us,
        care for us.
        And whatever surprises we encounter,
        hear us,
        comfort us,
        enfold us,
        give us peace.   *Rupert Bristow*

123   Ever-faithful Lord,
        forgive our forgetfulness, whenever and wherever it occurs.
        And in our old age help us to focus on you,
        even when other things are unclear to us.
        May the residual memories and knowledge of you
        break out of the cloud of unknowing
        and set us free.   *Rupert Bristow*

124   Eternal Father,
        your Son taught us the importance of things that last
        and the transience of the material world.
        In the dementia that afflicts those of all ages,
        but especially the elderly,
        give hope and flashes of clarity
        amid the fog of forgetfulness.
        Let the spirit of your presence
        be evident in the hearts of those affected,
        even if it is hidden from our sight.   *Rupert Bristow*

125   Great and glorious God,
      let the translucence of your presence
      always show through the hesitations and repetitions of
      dementia.
      May our patience and perception
      not be found wanting,
      as we seek the person within, and the spirit of faith,
      in gesture and twinkle, in touch and gaze,
      guided by your bright star. *Rupert Bristow*

126   God of spirit and truth,
      may the practice of the Eucharist
      break through barriers of memory,
      as we give thanks through bread and wine.
      Let those with all their frailties intact
      be especially sensitive to those whose gifts are restricted.
      May we always respect the person,
      as your Son respected all. *Rupert Bristow*

127   Lord of life,
      renew in us a right spirit,
      toward stranger and sufferer,
      as well as neighbor and friend.
      We never know when illness will strike,
      gradually or all at once.
      Let us look out for the needs
      and struggles of those with dementia,
      not through enlightened self-interest,
      but through love of humankind,
      love of your creation. *Rupert Bristow*

128   Lord of unity and diversity,
      what you have brought together
      may sometimes be put asunder,
      given our fallen state.
      We ask your forgiveness and patience,
      long-suffering Lord.
      We ask for the second chance
      that you gave to humankind,
      through your Son. *Rupert Bristow*

129   God of justice and mercy,
       look down on the imperfection of humankind,
       breathe a sigh, shed a tear,
       and help us to face up to divorce,
       if that is the only way forward.
       May repentance and forgiveness
       be the right way to part
       and the only way to move on.   *Rupert Bristow*

130   Lord of love,
       we have let you down
       when a marriage crumbles.
       Help us to shoulder blame and responsibility,
       if we have contributed
       to the pressure and pain of separation.
       But let us also take the responsibility
       of mending lives,
       through prayer, through listening,
       through being there for people,
       in the hope of reconciliation,
       in the expectation of a second chance.   *Rupert Bristow*

131   God of peace,
       we lift up to you
       all those who are victims of domestic violence,
       who suffer in silence
       and simmer in resentment.
       May they have the courage to resist assertively
       and report or raise the alarm.
       May bullies never prosper
       where you are Lord of all.   *Rupert Bristow*

132   Savior God, Prince of peace,
       may we always be aware
       of the early warnings of domestic violence,
       in ourselves and in those we love.
       Help us to head off growing resentment
       and ensure that differences are talked through
       without resorting to raised voices or raised hands.

May the sun never set
without a resolution of resentments.
And let the power of prayer and contemplation
always be preferable to instant reaction,
done or said in anger.
Help us to respect and forgive in an atmosphere of calm,
just as we pray to you in the midst of turmoil.
Rupert Bristow

133   God of our fathers,
send us the hope of reconciliation
after the despair of aggression.
Let domestic dispute lead to domestic understanding,
without the oppression of the cycle of destruction,
which can turn reason to unreason,
sweetness to bitterness,
discussion to violence.
Cast out violence from our nature,
transforming Lord.
Rupert Bristow

134   God of first and last,
may reason be first and violence be last
in our repertoire of response.
Let self-defense prevent the worst
and may assertiveness and the art of listening
calm emotion and avoid escalation.
Rupert Bristow

135   Transforming Lord,
send us out in sympathy
for those who experience domestic violence.
Send us out in confidence
to cope with perpetrators of violence.
Safeguard us from danger,
but let us not shrink
from saying things that challenge unacceptable behavior,
knowing that your Son upset the tables of the moneychangers,
but did not countenance violence to people,
except when he accepted humankind's violence to him.
Rupert Bristow

136   God of steadfast love,
      save us from the diversion of drugs,
      the insidious craving and the dependence.
      Let us be alert to the symptoms,
      in ourselves and in others,
      of a reliance on substances
      that cause addiction and damage.
      Lord of all,
      let us delight in trying new tastes,
      in sampling the fruits of your creation.
      But keep us from depending on anything or anyone,
      except you, as our guide,
      an ever-present help in trouble,
      and the source of all true joy.   *Rupert Bristow*

137   Savior, Servant, Sovereign,
      all things come from you,
      but you have given us the free will
      to consume too much
      and to fail to respect our bodies and our minds,
      so dishonoring you.
      Keep our hearts, minds, and bodies
      free from false gods, evil cravings,
      and, even when we fail,
      bring us back to you, we pray.   *Rupert Bristow*

138   Father of all,
      when we stray, pull us back;
      when we are on the edge, do not allow us to tip over; when
      we feel at the end of our rope,
      help us to realize that you are there at the other end,
      if we just acknowledge you
      and depend on no other.   *Rupert Bristow*

139   Lord God,
      set us free from drugs in all their forms.
      Help us to recognize, in ourselves and others around us,
      the telltale signs of absenteeism and introspection.

May those who battle with addiction
and those who confront the drug pushers and smugglers
have success as well as support
in their difficult tasks. *Rupert Bristow*

140   Gracious God,
reach out to our broken and bleeding world,
and bind up its wounds.
Reach out to those who are sorrowful and hurting,
and bring comfort deep within.
Reach out to all who walk through the valley of tears
and bring the assurance that those who mourn will one day laugh—
that, by your grace,
tears will give way to laughter,
and despair to delight. *Nick Fawcett*

141   Loving God,
we bring before you the sick and suffering of our world.
We pray for those afflicted in body:
racked by physical pain,
wrestling with disease,
enduring painful surgery,
or coming to terms with terminal illness.
We pray for those disturbed or troubled in mind:
those whose confidence has been crushed,
those no longer able to cope with the pressures of daily life,
those oppressed by false terrors of the imagination,
and those facing the dark despair of depression.
We pray for those afflicted in spirit:
all who feel their lives to be empty,
or whose beliefs are threatened,
or who have lost their faith,
or who have become caught up in superstition, black magic,
or the occult.
Living God,
reach out through all who work to bring wholeness and healing.
Support and strengthen them in their work.

Grant them wisdom and guidance,
strength and support,
and the ability to minister something of your care and compassion
for all.
In the name of Christ we ask it. *Nick Fawcett*

142   Lord Jesus Christ,
you spoke,
and you brought hope, comfort, and renewal;
you touched,
and you brought love, peace, healing, and wholeness.
Come now,
and speak again,
bringing your word of life to all who suffer or are hurting.
Reach out afresh,
bringing your touch of love to all whose hearts are aching
and who cry out for help.
Where there is despair and turmoil,
may your voice renew.
Where there is pain and sickness,
may your hand restore.
Lord Jesus Christ,
you came once,
you shall come again,
but we ask you,
come now,
and minister your grace,
for your name's sake. *Nick Fawcett*

143   Loving God,
we remember today all who mourn,
their hearts broken by tragedy,
tears a constant companion,
laughter and happiness seeming a distant memory.
Reach out into their pain, heartache, and sadness,
and give them the knowledge that you understand their hurt
and share their sorrow.

May your arms enfold them,
your love bring comfort,
and your light scatter the shadows,
so that they may know joy once more
and celebrate life in all its fullness. *Nick Fawcett*

144 God of all comfort,
we bring you this world of so much pain:
our own and that of those around us.
We bring you our hurts, troubles, anxieties, and fears,
placing them into your hands,
and we pray for those countless others facing sorrow or suffering:
hopes dashed,
dreams broken,
let down by those they counted dear;
betrayed,
abused,
wrestling with depression or illness,
mourning loved ones.
Hold on to us and to all who walk through the valley of tears.
Reach out and grant the knowledge that you are with us,
even there,
sharing our pain and moved by our sorrow.
Minister the consolation that you alone can offer,
and give the assurance that those who mourn will be comforted
and those who weep will laugh.
Lord,
in your mercy,
hear our prayer,
in Christ's name. *Nick Fawcett*

145 Loving God,
we pray for all who are bearing heavy burdens—
those facing difficulties and problems to which they can see no solutions,
wrestling with inner fears and phobias,
racked by anxiety for themselves or loved ones,
troubled about money, health, work, or relationships—
all who crave rest for their souls but cannot find it.

We pray for them and for ourselves,
acknowledging that sometimes we too feel crushed under a weight of care.
Speak to all in your still small voice,
and grant the peace and quiet confidence that only you can bring;
and so may burdens be lifted and souls refreshed.
Lord,
in your mercy,
hear our prayer,
in the name of Christ. *Nick Fawcett*

146 Lord Jesus Christ,
we remember today how, throughout your ministry,
you looked to bring healing and wholeness.
We remember how you touched the lepers,
restored sight to the blind,
cured the sick,
and helped the lame to walk;
how you brought hope to the broken-hearted
and those crushed in spirit,
peace of mind to those who were troubled,
and forgiveness to those burdened by guilt or failure.
Lord Jesus Christ,
we bring before you all in any kind of need,
praying again for your healing and renewing touch
in body, mind, and spirit,
this and every day.
Restore us and make us whole,
by your grace. *Nick Fawcett*

147 Compassionate God,
reach out into the sorrows, hurts,
disappointments, and regrets that we carry within us
and grant the comfort that you alone can bring.
Wipe away the tears,
tend the wounds,
and mend the brokenness of body, mind, and spirit,
through Jesus Christ our Lord. *Nick Fawcett*

148 Sovereign God,
   take our fragmented lives
   and, through your gracious touch,
   make us whole.
   Take our broken world
   and, through your sovereign grace,
   bring healing.
   Reach out to us and through us,
   in the name of Christ. *Nick Fawcett*

149 Lord Jesus Christ,
   take the bruised, battered, and broken pieces of our lives
   and, by your grace, put us together again. *Nick Fawcett*

150 Living God,
   teach us to bring our needs to you,
   knowing that,
   though you may not always respond as we want you to,
   you will always respond in love,
   providing for our needs,
   granting us peace, and making us whole.
   In the name of Christ we ask it. *Nick Fawcett*

151 God of grace,
   breathe health into our bodies,
   love into our hearts,
   peace into our minds,
   and joy into our spirits.
   Send us out now,
   made new, made whole,
   to live life fully as you desire.
   In Christ's name we ask it. *Nick Fawcett*

152 Lord Jesus Christ,
   touch the raw spots in our lives,
   the aching places deep within,
   and bring us the healing and wholeness
   that you alone can give,
   through your gracious love. *Nick Fawcett*

153   Living God,
       we bring not only the needs of others but also our own,
       for we are all in some way bruised,
       troubled in body, mind, or spirit.
       Reach out then to all—
       restoring, renewing, holding, healing—
       and teach us to reach out also,
       not as the strong to the weak
       or the healthy to the sick,
       but as fellow strugglers along the journey of life,
       in common need of the help and wholeness
       that you desire for all.   *Nick Fawcett*

154   Loving God,
       teach us that,
       though our bodies may be broken,
       our minds battered and our spirits crushed,
       you still see and value us as whole people,
       and, in that knowledge,
       may we find inner healing and tranquility,
       until that day when you make us new in your eternal kingdom,
       through Jesus Christ our Lord.   *Nick Fawcett*

155   Living God,
       we don't want to neglect our body, for it is your gift,
       but what of our soul, the inner-self?
       Teach us to seek wholeness of spirit with equal resolve,
       to work for true well-being,
       cultivating a health that will neither fade nor perish.
                                                     Nick Fawcett

156   Loving Lord,
       you are always looking to respond to our needs,
       constantly reaching out to touch our lives with your love,
       yet all too often we fail to seek the help you long to give us.
       We trust in our own strength;
       we try this, that, and everything else;

and we only remember you when we reach the end of
our rope
and there is no one left to turn to.
Forgive us for relegating you to the periphery
rather than putting you at the center of our lives.
Forgive us for treating you as a last resort instead of a
first recourse.
Teach us to bring our needs to you,
knowing that, though you may not always respond as we
want you to,
you will always respond in love,
providing for our needs,
granting us peace,
and bringing us the wholeness that you alone can give.
In your name we ask it. *Nick Fawcett*

157 Living God,
we like to think that we are the world's survivors,
able to meet whatever life may throw at us and
emerge unscathed,
but, in our hearts of hearts,
we know that we are as vulnerable as the next person,
our composure and confidence hanging on a thread
that can be broken at any time.
A crisis,
difficulty,
disappointment,
or personal tragedy,
and the whole edifice we have so carefully constructed
can come tumbling down around our ears.
Most of the time we succeed in shutting out such thoughts,
finding them too uncomfortable to contemplate,
but sometimes they force their way into our consciousness,
and we can escape them no longer.
Save us from running away in a vain attempt to deny
the truth;
from taking a road that leads only to uncertainty mounting
and fear gaining an ever-firmer hold.

Teach us instead to share our burdens and anxieties with you,
and so to find strength,
peace,
hope,
and courage,
even when the storm rages about us,
secure in the knowledge of your eternal love
made known through Jesus Christ our Lord. *Nick Fawcett*

158 Loving God,
we know what we should be and we know what we are,
the gulf between the two so wide.
So we come now in shame and sorrow before you,
seeking your mercy.
Forgive us everything that disfigures our life:
the pride, greed, selfishness, and envy
that alienate us not only from ourselves and others
but also, and above all,
from you.
Forgive us our unkind words,
foolish deeds,
and unworthy thoughts;
our weakness of will
and carelessness in discipleship.
Work within us
and, by your grace,
make us whole,
through Jesus Christ our Lord. *Nick Fawcett*

159 Lord,
it isn't easy to face the truth
for there is much we prefer to hide
from ourselves as well as others.
We are ashamed of our many failings—
the way we so easily succumb to temptation
and so often fail to honor you.
We talk of strength,
but show weakness.

We speak of serving others,
but have time only for ourselves.
We preach forgiveness,
but are swift in practice to judge.
Though we have caught a glimpse of what life could be
the reality is that we fall pathetically short,
yet we keep up a façade for the world rather than admit
the facts.
Lord,
you see us as we are,
for there can be nothing hidden from you,
and yet still you love us.
Give us courage, then, to face ourselves honestly,
and to acknowledge our faults,
so that we may know the forgiveness you offer
and rejoice in the renewal of life,
through Jesus Christ our Lord.   *Nick Fawcett*

160   Gracious God,
once more we thank you for the wonder of your love
and the awesome extent of your mercy.
We have failed you in so much,
repeatedly ignoring your will and breaking your
commandments,
yet, despite our betrayal,
you not only forgive but also put our mistakes behind us.
However often we go astray,
however great our faults,
and however feeble the love we show in return,
you are always willing to forget and move on.
Teach us the secret of such love.
Touch our hearts with your goodness
and so may we learn to let go of past hurts
and build instead for the future.
May we be agents of your healing, redeeming, and renewing
grace,
to the glory of your name.   *Nick Fawcett*

161 Gracious God,
   though we try to put the past behind us,
   all too often we are haunted by mistakes.
   Though we try to make amends for the wrongs we've done,
   we find it hard to escape a sense of guilt.
   Remind us that you are always ready to offer free and total forgiveness,
   no matter how foolish we have been
   or how many opportunities we have wasted.
   Teach us that the past is done with
   and the future is open before us.
   Receive, then, our thanks and lead us forward,
   in the name of Christ. *Nick Fawcett*

162 Living God,
   though we have let you down in so many ways,
   teach us that you do not judge as we do,
   but that you are truly willing to forgive and forget.
   Teach us to put the past behind us
   and to accept the new life you so freely offer,
   and so may we live each day as your gift,
   nurtured by the love of Christ
   and renewed through your Holy Spirit,
   to your praise and glory. *Nick Fawcett*

163 Living God,
   when we look at our lives,
   we see so much that is wrong
   and so little that is right.
   We see selfishness and greed,
   envy and bitterness,
   rather than the fruits of the Spirit that we so much long to show.
   We see narrowness of mind,
   weakness of faith, and feebleness of commitment
   rather than the vision, trust, and dedication that you expect from us.
   We want to live and work for you,
   yet we seem incapable of doing so,
   and we despair of ever changing.

Help us to remember that you can achieve
what we cannot hope to do by ourselves;
that you love us and died for us even before we knew you.
Teach us that you believe in us,
even when we don't.
In Christ's name we pray. *Nick Fawcett*

164   Living God,
we thank you that you provide us not only with daily bread
but also with the bread of life—
inner nourishment that means we need never go spiritually
hungry again.
You offer us so much through which to nourish our faith:
your love in Christ,
the inner presence of your Holy Spirit,
and the testimony of the scriptures—
and yet all too often we fail to feed ourselves as we should.
The result is that we grow weak instead of strong,
our faith starved,
emaciated,
wasting away—
a pale shadow of what it ought to be.
Forgive us,
and teach us to nurture our faith
so that we may be strong in your service,
to your glory. *Nick Fawcett*

165   Lord Jesus Christ,
you know that we want to follow you,
but you know also how hard we find it to do so.
Despite our good intentions,
we repeatedly slip back into our old ways,
pursuing our own ends rather than your will.
Instead of working and witnessing for you,
we are lukewarm in service and weak in discipleship.
Instead of growing,
our faith has become stale and tired,
no longer challenging or inspiring us
as in the days when we first believed.

Forgive us for falling away so easily.
Cleanse, renew, and restore us by your redeeming touch,
and help us to live for you today, tomorrow, and every day,
sure and steadfast,
to the glory of your name. *Nick Fawcett*

166 Gracious God,
we thank you that you are always with us,
in the bad times as well as the good,
the difficult as well as the easy,
the sad as well as the happy.
We thank you that
though we have sometimes been unsure of the way ahead,
you have always been there to guide us;
though we have felt discouraged,
you have offered us fresh inspiration;
though we have been in despair,
yet you have given us hope.
Through all the changing circumstances of life,
we have found from personal experience
that your steadfast love never ceases
and that your mercies are new every morning.
May the knowledge of all you have done
give us confidence in the days ahead,
so that whatever problems we face,
whatever disappointments we experience,
whatever sorrows may befall us,
we will still find reason to look forward,
reason to believe in the future,
and reason to hope.
Lord of all hopefulness,
hear our prayer,
in the name of Christ. *Nick Fawcett*

167 Lord,
it is hard sometimes not to lose faith in your purpose.
When hopes are dashed,
when dreams are shattered,
when one disappointment piles up on another,
it's difficult not to lose heart completely,
not to retreat into a shell of despair.

We want to believe we can change,
but there seems little evidence to support it.
We want to believe the world can be different,
but experience appears to prove otherwise.
Our hearts tells us one thing,
our head says another,
and the latter finally wins the day.
Yet you have promised that nothing in heaven or on earth
will finally overcome your purpose,
and throughout history you have shown that to be true,
constantly overturning human expectations,
hope returning like a phoenix from the ashes.
Speak to us now through the faith and vision of those who
have gone before,
so that, however dark the world may seem,
we too may dare to hope in turn,
through Jesus Christ our Lord. *Nick Fawcett*

168 Light of the world,
shine wherever there is darkness today.
Where there is pain and sorrow,
may the brilliance of your love bring joy.
Where there is sickness and suffering,
may your healing touch bring sunshine after the storm.
Where there is greed and corruption,
may your radiance scatter the shadows.
Where there is hatred and bitterness,
may your brightness dispel the clouds.
Lord Jesus Christ,
light of the world,
rise again upon us we pray,
and illuminate the darkness of this world
through your life-giving grace.
In your name we ask it. *Nick Fawcett*

169 Gracious God,
we read in Scripture of good news for the poor
and liberty for the oppressed,
yet sometimes the reality appears very different.

Day after day,
we hear stories of poverty, sickness, sorrow, and suffering—
some from far afield,
some on our own doorstep.
All around us there seems to be so much injustice and
oppression,
hatred and evil.
We try to trust in your purpose,
but the reality of this world seems to belie your will
and contradict the gospel.
Reach out, we pray, wherever there is need,
and grant that the light of your love may shine in our hearts
and in the hearts of all,
to the glory of your name. *Nick Fawcett*

170 Loving God,
hear our prayer for the have-nots of this world:
those who have no homes,
living as refugees or rough on our streets;
those who have no food,
their crops having failed,
their economies burdened by debt,
or their labors not fairly rewarded;
those who have no fresh water,
daily facing the threat of disease and the nightmare
of drought;
those who have insufficient resources to help themselves,
condemned to a life of poverty with no prospect of respite;
those who have no access to education, a health service,
or welfare system;
no one to turn to for help or support.
Loving God,
stir the hearts of all to work for a fairer world
and a more just society.
Challenge all who have plenty to respond to those who have
little,
so that all may share in the riches of your creation
and be able to celebrate your gift of life.
In Christ's name we ask it. *Nick Fawcett*

171 Loving God,
    we pray for all who are lonely:
    those whose relationships have been broken
    or who have never enjoyed the relationships they might have had;
    those who feel rejected by society and unsure of their worth;
    those who spend day after day alone
    and those who feel hopelessly isolated even when they are in company.
    Give to each one the knowledge that you are with them always,
    and enrich their lives with companionship and friendship.
    In the name of Christ we ask it. *Nick Fawcett*

172 Eternal God,
    we try to walk the way of Christ, but we repeatedly slip up,
    temptation and weakness causing us to flounder,
    and before we know it we find ourselves back where we started,
    the journey of discipleship proving more demanding
    than we ever imagined.
    Guide our footsteps, so that we may tread the path of faith more surely.
    And should we slide backwards,
    take us by the hand and lead us forward again. *Nick Fawcett*

173 Almighty God,
    when we're drained by the rat-race of life,
    wearied by its ceaseless demands,
    renew our strength, and help us to go the extra mile.
    However tough the challenge may be,
    however demanding the course,
    give us the help we need to meet it. *Nick Fawcett*

174 Creator God,
    heal our broken world, and put an end to its madness,
    so that, whatever divides,
    and whatever our color, creed, or culture,
    we may see beyond cause or grievance
    to the common humanity that unites us all. *Nick Fawcett*

175   Lord Jesus Christ,
       despised and rejected during your ministry,
       reach out to the marginalized—
       those pushed to the edge of society,
       their identity denied, rights ignored, and dignity destroyed.
       Overcome the barriers of fear, suspicion, and prejudice that divide us,
       estranging person from person,
       community from community,
       and, whatever our differences,
       help us to recognize the true worth of all—
       to see beyond what keeps us apart
       to the common humanity that binds us together.
                                                 Nick Fawcett

176   Living God,
       we pray for those who find faith hard,
       those who want to believe but cannot get past their doubts.
       We pray for those whose faith is wavering,
       undermined by the pressures and temptations of life.
       We pray for those who have lost their faith,
       the fire that once burned within them extinguished.
       We pray for ourselves,
       conscious that for us too faith can sometimes lose its spark.
       For all those whose faith is faltering we pray:
       "Lord, we do believe,
       help us overcome our unbelief."   *Nick Fawcett*

177   Living God,
       we know what our lives ought to be like,
       we know what they are,
       and we are ashamed at the difference between the two.
       Where we ought to reveal Christ,
       we show only ourselves.
       Where we ought to bear witness to his life-changing power,
       we demonstrate instead how little has actually changed.
       So much about us denies rather than affirms the gospel,
       leading people to dismiss its claims
       rather than to explore them further.

Forgive us for all that is wrong
and, by your Spirit, clothe us with joy,
peace,
patience,
kindness,
generosity,
faithfulness,
gentleness,
self-control,
and, above all, love.
Work in our lives,
and so work through us to speak to others,
through the grace of Christ. *Nick Fawcett*

178   Lord Jesus Christ,
just as you brought new out of old
through your fulfillment of the Law and the prophets,
so also continue to make us new,
taking our old self and refashioning it by your grace
into a new creation.
Help us to let go of everything in our past that denies
and destroys,
separating us from your love.
Take what we are and re-create us by your power,
so that we may be the people you would have us be,
for we ask it in your name. *Nick Fawcett*

179   Lord Jesus Christ,
we are not good at letting go of the past,
at recognizing there are times when we need to move on
in life;
to take a step forward in faith if we are ever truly to grow.
We prefer the security of the familiar,
the comfort of that which does not stretch or challenge us
too far,
and we are wary of the prospect of change,
afraid that it might ask more of us than we are willing
to give.

We are not good at letting go of the old and putting on the new,
at turning away from our former way of life
and taking instead the way of the cross.
We are reluctant to abandon old habits,
fearful of being thought different,
unwilling to deny ourselves the pleasures of this world
for the promise of the world to come.
So we try to keep a foot in both camps,
to combine the old self with the new.
We think we can balance the two,
but, of course, we can't,
and the result is that we compromise both
and embrace neither.
Help us to understand that, while the old has its place,
there are some areas in life where a complete break is needed,
a turning away from what has been,
before we are ready to receive what shall be.
Lord Jesus Christ,
you want to work within us to finish the new creation you have begun.
Give us courage to trust you completely,
so that you may refashion our lives to your glory.
We ask it in your name.
Nick Fawcett

180   Gracious God,
we don't have to tell you how weak is our prayer life,
for you know it already,
or how weak is our faith,
for you can see that clearly.
We are afraid to pin too many hopes on prayer,
in case you do not grant our requests.
We are hesitant to ask, in case we are seeking the wrong things.
Teach us that you are a God who listens and delights
to respond.

Save us from the lack of trust that frustrates your purpose,
preventing us from recognizing your hand at work.
Give us ears to hear,
eyes to see,
and hearts that truly believe,
through Jesus Christ our Lord.

Nick Fawcett

181 Lord Jesus Christ,
we know that God hears our prayers,
that he is ready to answer when we call to him,
but we are still reluctant sometimes to ask for help,
for we are conscious of having asked so many times before.
We seek forgiveness for the same old mistakes.
We ask for answers to the same old problems.
We look for guidance concerning the same old matters.
We intercede for the same old people.
Day after day,
week after week,
we bring the same list of requests,
so familiar that even we have grown tired of them,
let alone him.
We are afraid of exhausting his patience,
of becoming an irritation and a nuisance,
and we wonder whether we are asking for the wrong things,
or whether perhaps God has given his answer,
only we have failed to hear.
Yet you tell us he is always ready to listen,
always wanting to bless,
and that no matter how often we approach him
he will make time to hear us and time to answer.
Teach us, then, to approach with confidence
and to bring all our needs in faith before him,
assured that he longs to meet our need
and that, in the fullness of time,
he will respond.
In your name we ask it.

Nick Fawcett

182 Gracious God,
    you call us to support one another,
    to offer comfort in times of need,
    reassurance in times of fear,
    inspiration in times of challenge,
    and confidence in times of doubt.
    Forgive us for so easily doing the opposite—
    finding fault,
    running down,
    criticizing, and condemning.
    Forgive us for seeing the worst instead of the best,
    for believing the bad instead of the good,
    for so often pulling down and so rarely building up.
    Teach us to recognize people's gifts and nurture them,
    to understand their problems and share them,
    to acknowledge their successes and applaud them,
    to appreciate their efforts and affirm them.
    Teach us, through the faith we show in people,
    to help them attempt great things and expect great things;
    to look at life seeing not the obstacles but the opportunities,
    not the things they can't do but the things they can.
    So may we help them in Christ to discover their gifts,
    recognize their true worth and fulfill their potential,
    through his grace.   *Nick Fawcett*

183 Living God,
    sometimes we feel weighed down
    by the stresses and strains of daily life—
    oppressed by worry,
    unable to throw off our anxieties,
    held captive by a multitude of secret fears.
    We thank you for all those who help us through
        such moments,
    who offer a shoulder to lean on,
    an arm to steady, and a hand to share the load.
    Teach us in turn to bear the burdens of others,
    doing all we can through listening,
    understanding,
    caring, and sharing,
    to offer them our help.

As you have reached out to us,
so teach us to reach out in turn,
expressing your love and showing your care,
to the glory of your name. *Nick Fawcett*

184 Sovereign God,
there is so much in our lives that separates us from you
and others—
our selfishness, pride, greed, and envy;
our thoughtless actions,
foolish words, and selfish nature;
our narrowness of outlook and blinkered preconceptions—
so much that runs contrary to your will and denies
your love.
We thank you that, through Jesus,
you have broken down the barriers that divide person
from person
and humanity from you.
Help us and all your people to live in such a way
that we reflect this truth in all we are and do.
Stir the hearts of all,
so that the day may come
when the worth of everyone will be recognized,
their rights observed,
their dignity respected,
and their good pursued.
In Christ's name we ask it. *Nick Fawcett*

185 Father God,
reach out to all who are lonely,
deprived of human companionship through age or
infirmity,
or separated from others—
even when they are with them—
through fear,
shyness,
mistrust, or prejudice.

Reach out into our fragmented society,
in which so much of the feeling of community has been lost,
where ties that once bound families together have been broken,
where so many live only for themselves.
Father,
give to us and to all a sense of worth
and an understanding of the humanity that binds us together,
through Jesus Christ our Lord. *Nick Fawcett*

186 Healing God,
bring closer the day when our divisions will be overcome,
our differences put aside, and our fear and mistrust ended—
a time when we will live in peace together,
and you will be all in all. *Nick Fawcett*

187 Living God, to all who seek pleasure through intoxication, blotting out perception to fill the void within, grant genuine fulfillment. Pour into their hearts the sparkling wine of your love that they may find true life, their cup spilling over, full to overflowing. *Nick Fawcett*

188 Lord Jesus Christ, reach out to all who, seeking freedom and fulfillment, abuse their bodies to escape them; all who, in their search for happiness, are vulnerable to unscrupulous predators. Help them to get a buzz out of life not through artificial means, chemically induced elation, but through experiencing the thrill of your presence, and tasting the inner ecstasy that you alone can bring. *Nick Fawcett*

189 Eternal God, hear our prayer for those in their twilight years, the sun beginning to set though yet not gone down. Though the energy of youth is long past and aspirations of middle years seem distant, may this time of life bring joys of its own: an inner tranquility and contentment in light of all that has gone before, coupled with confident trust in what is yet to come—the new dawn that, by your grace, will surely follow the night. *Nick Fawcett*

190   Gracious God, when strength fails and faculties diminish, advancing years taking their toll, remind us that you bring new beginnings, life that will never fade. *Nick Fawcett*

191   Loving God, reach out to those who have lost the will to live, all who are broken in body, mind, or spirit, seeing no hope, no future, no reason to continue. Lift their despair, and may they find in you a life that satisfies, now and always. *Nick Fawcett*

192   Savior Christ, so many in life are worn to breaking point, ground down by sickness, hurt, worry, and fear, by the ravages of time, and uncertain how much longer they can cope. Reach out to strengthen and restore, from the tangled threads of their lives weaving cords that will not be broken. *Nick Fawcett*

193   Lord Jesus Christ, as you touched the untouchables throughout your ministry, so you reach out still, seeing not the affliction but the person underneath. Forgive the feebleness of our love, and teach us to do the same. *Nick Fawcett*

194   Loving God, when hearts are broken, lives wrecked by sickness, fear, hurt, and sorrow, people can break down completely, the business of repair a long and uncertain business. Reach out to all who feel they cannot carry on, and give them strength not just to resume their journey but to embark on it with confidence renewed and anticipation restored, able to see it safely through until they reach the end. *Nick Fawcett*

195   Lord Jesus Christ, when love brings hurt, the pain of rejection, betrayal, or loss, may your love bring comfort, and help to heal the wounds. *Nick Fawcett*

196 Renewing God, so many find their lives shattered—broken by the loss of a loved one, accident or injury, the onset of disease or the breakdown of relationships—and though sometimes they can be restored and the pieces put back together, sometimes they can't, in this life, at least, the damage being too great to mend. Reach out into fragmented hearts, bringing healing and hope, until that day when your kingdom comes, and all is made whole.
Nick Fawcett

197 Loving God, our world lies broken, fractured by prejudice, splintered by hate, scarred by fear, and for all our efforts we cannot make it whole. Pick up the pieces and bind them together, bringing healing where there is hurt and unity where there is division. Hear our prayer and honor our hopes.
Nick Fawcett

198 Lord Jesus Christ, reach out to our broken world—scarred by hatred, fractured by division, ravaged by war—and, in your mercy, grant us peace.
Nick Fawcett

199 Merciful God, thank you for the knowledge that you are always there, ready to carry us when we cannot continue, to tend to our wounds when we lie bruised and broken, to provide healing and renewal in body, mind, and spirit. Teach us to minister to life's casualties in turn, reaching out with supportive hands and caring touch, in your name.
Nick Fawcett

200 Loving God, we see news pictures day after day of hunger, squalor, violence, and suffering beamed into our living rooms from across the world, and our hearts go out to those enduring such misery. But we are able to turn away, dismissing such things from our minds. Only there's no such option for them: this is the daily reality of their lives. Remind us that they are real people, each one our neighbor, and instead of pushing them aside, as if they are part of another world, teach us, whenever and wherever we can, to respond in love.
Nick Fawcett

201   Holy God, our world is stained, engulfed by a black tide of injustice, intolerance, fear, and hatred that desecrates and destroys countless lives and, for all our so-called advances, we're no nearer containing it than we've ever been. Come to our aid, and cleanse us of all that denies and divides—that precludes joy and crushes hope. Transform what we can never change ourselves, and make all things new.
Nick Fawcett

202   Lord of all, overcome the barriers that keep us apart, dividing person from person and race from race—East and West, black and white, male and female, rich and poor. Whatever our color, culture, or creed, draw us together and heal our wounds—so that we may live and work together as one people, one world.
Nick Fawcett

203   Lord of the nations, when we consider the scale of human need, the enormous suffering, injustice, and deprivation faced by so many, we feel despondent, overwhelmed, for we seem powerless to change anything, to do anything meaningful to help. The world is so big, and we are so small, insignificant in terms of the forces that shape and control it. Help us, nonetheless, in our living and loving, our speaking and doing, to work for change, in partnership with you and others. Remind us that what we can't do, you can.
Nick Fawcett

204   Renewing God, grant not just superficial peace in our world, but reconciliation, an end to whatever divides and destroys—all that fosters hatred, intolerance, and injustice leading to misery for so many. Break down religious, ethnic, and social barriers, so that those previously estranged may come together, moving beyond their differences to a genuine meeting of minds, and harmony among all.
Nick Fawcett

205   Loving God, reach out to our broken world—scarred by suspicion, fractured by hatred, ravaged by cruelty, violence, and war—and, in your mercy, heal our wounds, overcome our divisions, and grant us real and lasting peace.
Nick Fawcett

206 Loving God, reach out to the incapacitated—those injured through accident, wounded in war, maimed through illness, or deformed at birth. Equip them to face the challenges life brings, and to see themselves, however disfigured they may be, as whole people, precious in your sight.
Nick Fawcett

207 Eternal God, to all wrestling with terminal illness, give the assurance that you will always value them for who they are; and help their families, friends, and colleagues, as they struggle to come to terms with their feelings, to do the same, seeing not the illness but the individual underneath. Whatever else may be lost, may that continue, to the end and beyond.
Nick Fawcett

208 Lord Jesus Christ, hear our prayer for the sick—all who are in pain, waiting for or recovering from surgery, undergoing treatment or coming to terms with terminal illness. Give help and strength to any whose health is failing, and to all who tend to them.
Nick Fawcett

209 Compassionate God, forgive us, for we forget those who live in constant pain, longing for release yet finding no end to their suffering, each day blighted by its stranglehold. Give them strength not just to get through but also to find Joy and fulfillment in life, and grant the assurance that, just as you shared our sufferings in Christ, so, through him, we will all finally enter a brighter kingdom in which pain and sorrow will be at an end.
Nick Fawcett

210 Loving God, for those troubled about their health, and those with the responsibility of ministering to them, grant your help, guidance, and love.
Nick Fawcett

211 Lord Jesus Christ, who shed your blood for all, thank you for those who donate theirs to others in turn, from so simple an offering coming so special a gift to so great a multitude. Inspire us, if we are able, to do the same.
Nick Fawcett

212 God of grace and mercy, reach out to all in the hospital: the sick and frail; those waiting for an operation, fearful about the procedure or the future; those recovering from major surgery, wrestling with chronic disease, or struggling with pain; those coming to terms with terminal illness. Work through nurses, doctors, surgeons, and support staff, through counselors, ministers, friends, and family, and, through your Holy Spirit, to bring comfort, strength, relief, and healing. Through your love and that of others, grant to all facing ill health the knowledge that they are not alone.
Nick Fawcett

213 Healing God, hear our prayer for the sick—all who are in pain, waiting for or recovering from surgery, undergoing long-term treatment, battling against disease, anxious about the future. Support them through family and friends, through the skill and dedication of medical staff, and, above all, through the knowledge of your love. Minister your healing touch, and grant them the peace and strength they need to find wholeness in you.   *Nick Fawcett*

214 Loving God, overhaul our lives, and make us new. Recharge our batteries and clear away whatever prevents us from realizing our true potential. So work within us that we may not just get by, but live each moment to the fullest.
Nick Fawcett

215 Lord of all, rekindle in us the flame of hope and fire of expectancy, in the knowledge that, with you, however old we might be, life has always only just begun.   *Nick Fawcett*

216 Almighty God, we're not as strong as we like to think, the burdens of life sometimes being too heavy to bear. Thank you that when we cannot carry them alone, you are always there to share the load, nothing being too hard for you to shoulder.   *Nick Fawcett*

217 Living God, we feel drained sometimes, fit for nothing, reserves run dry. Yet you are a God of power, revitalizing the spirit, renewing strength. Flow into our hearts, and out through our lives. *Nick Fawcett*

218 Mighty God, when work piles up, weighing heavily upon us, give us wisdom to take things one step at a time, lest we collapse under the weight of it all and end up achieving nothing. *Nick Fawcett*

219 Lord Jesus Christ, when we're drained by the demands placed upon us, wearied to the point of exhaustion, renew our strength, and help us to go the extra mile. *Nick Fawcett*

220 Mighty God, thank you that when we're weary, the load too heavy to bear, you carry not just the burden, but us as well. *Nick Fawcett*

221 Father God, when we're at the end of our rope, our patience stretched to the limit, give us wisdom to recognize our limitations and grace to accept the constraints life puts upon us, before we reach the breaking point and something snaps. *Nick Fawcett*

222 We're tired, Lord, exhausted by the pressures of life, the daily demands that are placed upon us. Renew our strength, and help us to get through. *Nick Fawcett*

223 Gracious God, in many things, more than we realize, our pleasure comes at the expense of others, what brings us joy causes them pain. Teach us, in all we do, however innocent it may seem, to consider its impact on those around us, and, where necessary, to put their wishes before our own. *Nick Fawcett*

224 Lord Jesus Christ, forgive us, for we can cause discord more easily than we imagine, clashing with those around us and even with you. In all our relationships, help us to hit the right note; to be in tune with you, and, wherever possible, to live in harmony with others. *Nick Fawcett*

225 Teach us that the hurt people cause is not always intended, so much of what they say and do being an instinctive response rather than premeditated. Help us, then, when our instinct is to lash out and hurt in turn, to bear the wounds with grace, remembering how you so willingly were wounded for all in Christ. *Nick Fawcett*

226 Loving God, we don't know when to stop sometimes. Whether it's stealing a joke, testing someone's patience, taking liberties, or indulging to excess, we can push things too far and, though we may not see it, damage is done, greater than we might imagine. Whatever we start, help us to know when it's time to call a halt. *Nick Fawcett*

227 Lord Jesus Christ, teach us that we should simmer with rage about some things in life—injustice, exploitation, greed, hatred, and violence—but remind us also how easily anger can spill over into rage, destroying and wounding, adding to rather than alleviating the world's misery. Show us when it's right to be angry, but help us always to channel it, so that it will be a tool for good instead of evil.
Nick Fawcett

228 Father God, we forget that we need to switch off sometimes if we're not to end up exhausted. Teach us to appreciate the importance of being still, of taking a breather from the demands of life, however pressing they may be. Show us the difference between doing enough and doing too much, and help us to get the balance right. *Nick Fawcett*

229 Living God,
we pray for those people who have lost hope—
in their dreams,
their circumstances,
or in life itself.
Lord of all hopefulness,
hear our prayer.
We pray for those who have lost the hope
of finding a partner or of raising a family,
the hope of going to college, graduate school, or further studies,

the hope of finding a home
or any permanent roof over their heads,
the hope of securing employment or a use for their skills.
Lord of all hopefulness,
hear our prayer.
We pray for those who despair of seeing freedom,
justice, peace, or reconciliation;
those who despair of finding adequate food and clothing;
those who despair of receiving help and healing.
Lord of all hopefulness,
hear our prayer.
We pray for those who have given up on life—
those with terminal illness
who have lost the will to keep on fighting;
those whose spirits have been crushed
so that they can no longer bounce back;
those who want to take their own lives
because they have lost all hope;
those so afflicted by starvation and disease
that they cannot carry on.
Lord of all hopefulness,
hear our prayer.
Living God,
there is so much despair in our world,
and for many there seems little reason to hope.
Reach out, we pray, to all whose belief in the future
has been destroyed,
and grant new dreams where the old have died,
rekindled purpose where confidence has been undermined,
support when there seems to be nothing left to hold on to,
and hope that one day your kingdom will come
and your will be done.
Lord of all hopefulness,
hear our prayer,
in the name of Christ.

Nick Fawcett

230   Living God,
we pray for all those who are weighed down
by the stresses and strains of daily life—
those who long for peace of mind,
who crave rest for their souls,
but cannot find it.
Lord, in your mercy,
hear our prayer.
We pray for those oppressed by worry,
unable to throw off their anxieties,
held captive by a multitude of secret fears.
Lord, in your mercy,
hear our prayer.
We pray for those who cannot let go,
those who find it impossible to relax or unwind,
always fretting over this or that.
Lord, in your mercy,
hear our prayer.
We pray for those who lose themselves in busyness,
masking their true feelings
and running from their emptiness,
hoping that keeping active might bring them happiness.
Lord, in your mercy,
hear our prayer.
We pray for those who have lost time for you,
allowing the pressures and demands of each day
to shut you out,
putting any thought of you off until tomorrow.
Lord, in your mercy,
hear our prayer.
We pray for those who have no time for you,
no interest in anything other than their daily routine,
no awareness of their spiritual needs.
Lord, in your mercy,
hear our prayer.
Living God,
speak to each one in your still small voice,
and grant them your peace which passes understanding,
that quiet confidence which only you can bring,

and so may their burdens be lifted
and their souls refreshed.
Lord, in your mercy,
hear our prayer,
through Jesus Christ our Lord. *Nick Fawcett*

231 Loving God,
we pray for all those in our world
who knowingly take the path of evil—
those who follow a life of crime,
those who cheat and deceive,
who exploit their fellow human beings,
who wound in body or mind,
who kill and destroy.
Open their eyes to the reality of your judgment,
their minds to the damage caused by their actions,
and their hearts to the transforming power of your grace.
Lord, in your mercy,
hear our prayer.
Loving God,
we pray for those who are indifferent to you—
those who have not heard the challenge of the Gospel,
or who have not considered
the claims of Christ for themselves,
or who have a nominal faith but no real commitment.
Open their ears to the message of Christ,
their spirits to the reality of your presence,
and their lives to the joy of knowing you.
Lord, in your mercy,
hear our prayer.
Loving God,
we pray for those who seek to serve you,
but who find faith threatened—
those who face pain and suffering,
those overwhelmed by sudden calamity,
those confused by apparent injustice,
and those whose convictions have been undermined
by the experiences of life.

Assure them of your continuing purpose,
your enduring love,
and your final triumph.
Lord, in your mercy,
hear our prayer,
through Jesus Christ our Lord. *Nick Fawcett*

232 Sovereign God,
we pray for the weak and vulnerable in our world—
those who feel powerless
in the face of the massive problems that confront them.
Help of the helpless,
reach out to strengthen and support.
We pray for the poor,
the hungry,
the diseased,
the dying.
Help of the helpless,
reach out to strengthen and support.
We pray for the oppressed,
the exploited,
the abused,
the tortured.
Help of the helpless,
reach out to strengthen and support.
We pray for the frightened,
the lonely,
the hurt,
the depressed.
Help of the helpless,
reach out to strengthen and support.
We pray for those who live in lands racked by tension,
those who face famine and starvation,
those who are unemployed,
those who are homeless.
Help of the helpless,
reach out to strengthen and support.
Sovereign God,
you have expressed a special concern
for the bruised, the needy, and the weak of our world.

May that concern bring strength to all in such need,
and may it inspire people everywhere
to work for a more just society,
standing up for the needy,
and working for that time when there will be an end
to suffering, mourning, and pain;
that time when your kingdom will come
and your will be done.
Help of the helpless,
reach out to strengthen and support,
in the name of Christ.   *Nick Fawcett*

233 Loving God,
we pray for those whose dreams have been destroyed,
those who no longer have the heart to look forward,
who have lost their vision for the future.
So many people, known and unknown—
whose happiness and hopes have been dashed by tragedy,
whose faith in loved ones has been betrayed,
who face poverty, unemployment, homelessness,
disease, starvation, even death—
whose trust in you has been tested beyond the limit.
God of hope,
light a new flame in their hearts.
We pray for all those who plod wearily through life
with no sense of purpose—
those who feel the future is empty, bereft of promise,
and those who live only for today, fearful of tomorrow.
God of hope,
light a new flame in their hearts.
Touch their hearts, we pray,
stir their imagination,
rekindle their faith,
renew their hope.
And so may new dreams and new visions
be born in the most broken of lives.
God of hope,
light a new flame in their hearts,
through Jesus Christ our Lord.   *Nick Fawcett*

234   Living God,
    we pray for all those who feel
    they have lost control in their lives—
    overwhelmed perhaps by tragedy,
    or relationships having broken down;
    battling against the rigors of old age,
    or wrestling with terminal illness;
    in pain of body,
    or turmoil of mind.
    Lord of all,
    assure them that your purpose will finally win through.
    We pray for the victims of other people's lack of control,
    wounded in body or mind—
    abused children,
    battered wives,
    broken homes,
    victims of burglary, rape, or assault.
    Lord of all,
    assure them that your purpose will finally win through.
    We pray for those who struggle
    to control aspects of their character—
    lust,
    temper,
    greed,
    impatience,
    envy,
    intolerance.
    Lord of all,
    assure them that your purpose will finally win through.
    Living God,
    give to all near the end of their rope
    the assurance that you are ultimately in control;
    to those who are hurt
    the comfort of your healing love;
    to those troubled in mind
    the inner peace which you alone can give;
    and to those dismayed by their repeated failings
    the gift of self-control.
    Lord of all,
    assure them that your purpose shall finally win through,
    in the name of Christ our Lord.   *Nick Fawcett*

235 Living God,
we pray for those who face the future
with uncertainty or anxiety—
those who fear it,
who despair of it,
or who feel they have no future.
We pray for those in the troubled places of our world—
those who long for peace,
an end to conflict, and a time of harmony,
but who in their hearts have given up hoping.
We pray for those who face trauma
and upheaval in their lives—
what seemed secure swept from under them,
what they had hoped for denied them,
what they had trusted in proven false.
We pray for those who doubt their ability
to cope with what life may bring—
those overwhelmed by pressures,
paralyzed by fears,
crushed by sorrows.
We pray for those faced with difficult decisions—
circumstances beyond their control,
unexpected dangers,
awkward choices.
Living God,
reach out to all for whom the future
seems uncertain or unwelcome,
and bring the assurance that even in the darkest moments,
the greatest challenges,
the most worrying times,
you are there working out your purpose;
able to bring light out of darkness,
hope out of despair,
joy out of sorrow,
and good out of evil.
Grant the confidence that there is nothing in heaven or earth,
in life or death,
in the present or the future,
that is finally able to separate us from your love.
Through Jesus Christ our Lord. *Nick Fawcett*

236 Loving God,
we bring before you the sick and suffering of our world,
all those wrestling with illness in body, mind, or spirit.
Lord, in your mercy,
hear our prayer.
We pray for those afflicted in body—
enduring physical pain,
overwhelmed by disabling disease,
waiting for an operation or further treatment
and fearful of what the future may hold,
or living with the knowledge of a terminal illness.
Lord, in your mercy,
hear our prayer.
We pray for those disturbed or troubled in mind—
those whose confidence has broken down,
those unable to cope with the pressures of daily life,
those oppressed by false terrors of the imagination,
those facing the dark despair of clinical depression.
Lord, in your mercy,
hear our prayer.
We pray for those afflicted in spirit—
those who feel their lives to be empty,
or whose beliefs are threatened
or who have lost their faith,
or who worship gods of their own making
with no power to satisfy,
or whose hearts have become bitter and twisted,
and their minds dark.
Lord, in your mercy,
hear our prayer.
Living God,
we thank you for all who work
to bring help, wholeness, and healing to the sick—
doctors and nurses, surgeons and medical staff,
psychiatrists, counselors, clergy, and therapists.
Support and strengthen
all those who share in the work of healing,
all who strive to bring relief,
all who minister to others.

Lord, in your mercy,
hear our prayer.
Grant them your wisdom and guidance,
your care and compassion,
your strength and support.
Equip them in all they do,
and bring wholeness through them.
Lord, in your mercy,
hear our prayer.
Finally we pray for your Church
in the healing ministry you have called it to exercise,
an inner healing of body, mind, and soul
that only you can offer.
Grant that your people everywhere
may be so filled with your Holy Spirit,
and so touched by the grace of Christ,
that they may share effectively
in the wider work of healing,
through their life and witness
bringing wholeness to broken people
and a broken world.
Lord, in your mercy,
hear our prayer,
in the name of Christ.

Nick Fawcett

237 Lord Jesus Christ,
there are times when life seems a mystery,
when we can make no sense of anything,
not even our faith,
when the events of life confuse and trouble
us so that our minds are in turmoil
and our confidence is destroyed.
Help us to know you are with us at such times.
Speak again your word of peace,
and may our souls find rest.
Remind us of the experience of your followers
on that first Easter day—
how you came to them in their confusion—
each still reeling from the shock of your death,

struggling to come to terms with the suffering you had endured,
and the apparent triumph of evil over goodness—
and how you restored their faith,
rekindling their joy,
reviving their vision,
and renewing their commitment.
Speak again your word of peace,
and may our souls find rest.
We thank you for your promise to be with us always,
to the end of the age,
and we rejoice that we experience the fulfillment of those words
through the living presence of the Holy Spirit.
Whatever storms may confront us,
whatever trials we may face,
we know that you will always be there,
meeting us in our confusion to quieten our hearts.
Speak again your word of peace,
and may our souls find rest.
We thank you that the day will come
when your victory will be complete
and your will accomplished—
a day when the puzzles that confound us will be resolved,
when the forces that conspire against your kingdom
will be overcome,
and when harmony will be established among the nations—
a day when you will speak your word to all.
Speak again your word of peace,
and may our souls find rest.
Lord Jesus Christ,
meet with us when life is hard and our faith is weak,
and grant the assurance that, despite appearances,
your purpose continues unchanged,
your strength remains undiminished,
and your love is indestructible.
Speak again your word of peace,
and may our souls find rest.
We ask it in your name.

Nick Fawcett

238 Merciful God,
we pray for those who walk through life with a sense of guilt,
burdened by past mistakes,
overwhelmed by a sense of failure,
troubled by feelings of shame,
depressed by the knowledge of their own weakness.
Help them to understand that in you
they can find true forgiveness
and a new beginning.
Lord, in your mercy,
hear our prayer.
We pray for those who commit evil with no sense of wrongdoing,
no concept of sin,
no hint of remorse,
no sign of scruples.
Help them to glimpse what is right and good,
and to be touched by the renewing, transforming grace
of Christ.
Lord, in your mercy,
hear our prayer.
We pray for those who have been wronged by others—
those who have been hurt,
deceived,
betrayed,
let down.
Help them to be ready to forgive others as you have
forgiven us.
Lord, in your mercy,
hear our prayer.
We pray finally for one another,
in our relationships with family and friends,
in our relationships at work or leisure,
in our relationships in fellowship here,
and in our relationships with other Christians.
Help us to recognize any divisions or grievances
there may be between us,
and help us work toward the healing of all such rifts,
forgiving and seeking forgiveness.

Lord, in your mercy,
hear our prayer.
Merciful God,
help all in your world to discover the mercy you so
freely offer,
and to show that mercy in turn;
to be ready to put the past behind them,
and to begin again through your grace.
Lord, in your mercy,
hear our prayer.

Nick Fawcett

239   Loving God,
we bring to you our world of so much pain,
so much need and sorrow;
a world you care for so deeply
that you willingly gave your all for it,
living and dying among us through your Son, Jesus Christ.
Reach out again in mercy,
and heal our wounds.
We bring to you the causes of so much suffering—
the sin of greed,
denying the many their share of this earth's riches to the
benefit of the few;
the sin of waste,
wantonly squandering the resources you have given
with no thought of future generations;
the sin of intolerance,
dividing families, communities, and nations through
a refusal to engage in dialogue;
the sin of pride,
thinking too highly of ourselves and too poorly of others;
the sin of indifference,
caring too little about you, too little about anything.
Reach out again in mercy,
and heal our wounds.
We pray for those who pay the price of human folly—
the poor and the hungry,
the homeless and dispossessed,
victims of war and violence, crime and cruelty;

the distressed, isolated, crushed, and forgotten,
all who are deprived of love and denied hope.
Reach out again in mercy
and heal our wounds.
Loving God,
come again to our world
through your Son, our Savior.
Mend our divisions,
forgive our folly,
and guide all our affairs.
Reach out again in mercy,
and heal our wounds.
In the name of Christ we ask it. *Nick Fawcett*

240 Living God,
we thank you that you are a God who hears and answers prayer,
and we praise you for those times
when you have responded to us
and granted our requests.
But we confess that there are times, too, when you seem silent,
when, listen though we might, we cannot hear your voice.
And so we pray now for all who cry to you
but who feel their prayers are unanswered.
Lord, in your mercy, hear us,
and all who pray to you.
We think of those known to us facing difficult times—
battling with illness,
wrestling with depression,
anxious about the future,
grieving for loved ones—
those for whom life seems a puzzle,
even a burden,
and who long to find hope
to make some sense out of their confusion.
Lord, in your mercy, hear us,
and all who pray to you.

We think of those who feel far from you—
burdened by doubt,
overwhelmed by temptation,
crushed by failure—
those who long to know you better
but who find it hard to get close;
who seek to serve you
but who are weighed down by a sense of their weaknesses,
their lack of faith,
and their repeated mistakes.
Lord, in your mercy, hear us,
and all who pray to you.
We think of those who seek guidance—
who feel unsure of the way ahead,
uncertain of their ability to face that future,
unclear as to what you want from them,
or what you plan for their lives—
all who ask you to lead the way forward,
yet who still have no clear sense of their particular calling.
Lord, in your mercy, hear us,
and all who pray to you.
We think of the poor and the weak,
the vulnerable and disadvantaged in society—
those denied their rights,
their dignity,
their freedom,
their livelihoods—
all who long for a time when justice will be established
but who have given up believing it ever shall be.
Lord, in your mercy, hear us,
and all who pray to you.
Living God,
we are conscious that so many in our world cry out to you
yet seem to receive no answer—
some because they do not expect to receive any,
some because they are not ready or willing to listen,
some because they do not understand what you are saying,
but many genuinely and urgently longing to hear your voice,
yearning for some response.

Speak to them, we pray.
Do not keep silent,
but reach out into their pain and hurt,
their need and hopelessness,
and bring your word of comfort,
of peace,
of healing, love, and renewal.
Lord, in your mercy, hear us,
and all who pray to you.
In the name of Jesus Christ,
your Word made flesh.   *Nick Fawcett*

241 Almighty God,
we thank you for your great and never-ending love
which never stops seeking us out,
never fades,
and never lets us go.
We thank you for your care that we experience
every moment of every day,
for everything you have done for us and all the world
in Christ,
and we pray now for those who feel lonely,
unloved,
unwanted.
Lord, in your mercy,
reach out in love.
We pray for those whose relationships have been broken,
whether through separation, divorce, or bereavement;
and we pray for those who have never enjoyed
the relationships they might have had—
children unwanted by their parents,
parents alienated from children,
family members estranged from one another.
Lord, in your mercy,
reach out in love.
We pray for individuals who feel rejected by society—
those who have no confidence in their abilities,
no place where they feel accepted,
no sense of their own worth.

Lord, in your mercy,
reach out in love.
We pray for communities divided by prejudice, race, or religion,
for churches where there is disagreement,
tension, and disharmony,
and for nations broken by war and violence.
Lord, in your mercy,
reach out in love.
Almighty God,
bring friendship to the lonely,
reconciliation to the estranged,
harmony to the divided,
and comfort to the bereaved.
In our homes and our families,
our schools and our places of work,
our country and our world,
may your love be shared among us,
bringing hope and healing.
Lord in your mercy,
reach out in love.
In the name of Christ we ask it. *Nick Fawcett*

242 Living God,
we pray for all those who find faith difficult or impossible—
those beset by doubt,
troubled by questions to which they can find no answer,
unable to take the leap of faith,
yet seeking, searching, and thirsting for truth.
Lord, in your mercy,
hear our prayer.
We think of those unable to reconcile their own situations
with the claims of the gospel—
those whose dreams have been shattered,
their love betrayed,
their trust abused,
and their best efforts gone unrewarded.
Lord, in your mercy,
hear our prayer.

We think of those for whom events in the world at large
seem to deny your love—
those confronted by natural disaster,
sickened by war and violence,
dazed by sickness, suffering, and disease,
perplexed by the apparent victory in so many places
of evil over good.
Lord, in your mercy,
hear our prayer.
We pray also for those confirmed in their unbelief,
unwilling to consider further the claims of the gospel,
unmoved and unchallenged by the love of Christ.
Lord, in your mercy,
hear our prayer.
Living God,
break through the barriers of doubt and unbelief.
Open the hearts and minds
of all who are troubled and confused,
and all who are closed to your presence.
Meet with those who find it hard to meet with you,
and lead them to a living, life-giving faith.
Lord, in your mercy,
hear our prayer.
Through Jesus Christ our Lord. *Nick Fawcett*

243 Loving God,
we pray for those who are weary—
exhausted in body, mind, and soul.
Lord of life,
renew their strength and refresh their spirits.
We think of those whose daily work hangs heavy upon
them—
those in dull, soul-destroying employment,
in stressful and pressurized careers,
in labor that is heavy and physically exhausting,
or in jobs involving long and unsociable hours.
Lord of life,
renew their strength and refresh their spirits.
We think of those who have no job—
yearning for the opportunity to use their skills,

deprived of a sense of self-respect,
unable to provide for their loved ones as they would like to,
their life seeming empty and frustrating.
Lord of life,
renew their strength and refresh their spirits.
We think of those who are suffering—
battling against illness,
wrestling with infirmity,
crushed by physical disability,
or enduring long-term physical or emotional pain.
Lord of life,
renew their strength and refresh their spirits.
We pray for those who have lost their enthusiasm for life—
the depressed and downhearted,
the mentally disturbed,
the sad and disillusioned,
the frightened and anxious;
all those for whom just getting through another day
has become an effort.
Lord of life,
renew their strength and refresh their spirits.
We think of those who have nothing to sustain their hope—
those whose dreams have been crushed
by the harsh realities of life,
who struggle with doubt and uncertainty,
whose faith in you and the future
has been battered beyond repair,
their ability to bounce back finally exhausted.
Lord of life,
renew their strength and refresh their spirits.
Loving God,
draw near to all through Christ.
Grant the peace of your presence,
the healing of your touch,
the blessing of your guidance,
and the assurance of your constant love,
so that all who are weary may walk in hope
and look forward in faith.
Lord of life,
renew their strength and refresh their spirits.
Through Jesus Christ our Lord. *Nick Fawcett*

244 Lord of all,
  you have made us in your image,
  each one the work of your hands,
  a unique and precious creation,
  and we praise you for it.
  Yet we remember also how, across the centuries and still today,
  so many have endured prejudice and discrimination,
  rejected because of the color of their skin,
  persecuted due to their creed or culture.
  Reach out in love,
  and heal our divisions.
  Forgive the racism that still exists in our society—
  the automatic attaching of labels,
  the taunting and snide remarks,
  the denial of opportunities,
  the unconscious negative attitudes.
  Break down the barriers that divide our world,
  the ignorance and suspicion
  that inflict such pain on so many.
  Reach out in love,
  and heal our divisions.
  Forgive the racism that exists within ourselves,
  recognized or unrecognized—
  the naive assumptions and hidden biases—
  and forgive us those times we have remained silent
  when we should have spoken up,
  when we have ignored prejudice
  because we are personally unaffected.
  Help us to see each individual in their own right,
  and to appreciate their true worth.
  Reach out in love,
  and heal our divisions.
  We pray for all who experience racism—
  victims of verbal abuse or physical assault,
  of social exclusion, deprivation, and discrimination.
  Give them courage to hold their heads high,
  perseverance in standing up for their rights,
  and support in times of adversity.
  Reach out in love,
  and heal our divisions.

We pray finally for those who work for change—
campaigning for equality of opportunity,
striving to break down preconceptions,
building bridges across divided communities.
Encourage them in their efforts,
and grant that through bringing people together
prejudices may be overcome.
Reach out in love,
and heal our divisions.
Lord of all,
you have made us in your image,
each one the work of your hands,
a unique and precious creation.
Break down everything that comes between us,
and grant unity to our divided world,
and a proper respect for all.
Reach out in love,
and heal our divisions.
Through Jesus Christ our Lord. *Nick Fawcett*

245 Great and gracious God,
we pray for all those in life who carry heavy loads
and long for rest.
We pray for people weighed down by remorse,
carrying with them a burden of guilt—
those who have made mistakes,
who have said or done foolish things,
who have acted unthinkingly,
and who feel they can never find mercy.
Assure them of your constant forgiveness open to all.
Lord, in your mercy,
hear our prayer.
We pray for those weighed down
by a sense that life has lost its meaning,
carrying with them a burden of despair—
those who drift aimlessly through each day,
who look to the future with a sense of weariness,
who feel trapped in a rut from which there is no escape.
Assure them that you have a purpose for all.

Lord, in your mercy,
hear our prayer.
We pray for those weighed down by injustice,
carrying with them a burden of helplessness—
the poor, sick, and homeless,
the oppressed, persecuted, and wrongfully imprisoned—
all who are deprived of their basic human rights
and who feel powerless to do anything about it.
Assure them that you are able to transform all things,
however hopeless they may seem.
Lord, in your mercy,
hear our prayer.
We pray for those weighed down by advancing years,
carrying with them the burden of age—
those who wrestle with declining health,
who are confused by the pace of change,
who feel lonely and unloved,
or who grieve for old friends who have passed away.
Assure them that your word and love endure forever.
Lord, in your mercy,
hear our prayer.
We pray for those weighed down by the burden of doubt,
carrying with them a sense of shame
at having lost their faith—
those who feel cut off from you,
troubled by all kinds of questions,
unable to believe as they once did,
alone in a cold and empty world.
Assure them of your involvement in every part of life,
even when they cannot understand it.
Lord, in your mercy,
hear our prayer.
Great and gracious God
bring hope,
bring joy,
bring peace,
bring trust—
bring renewal of life
to all who struggle under heavy loads.

May they find in Christ the one whose yoke is easy
and whose burden is light,
and through him find rest for their souls.
Lord, in your mercy,
hear our prayer.
We ask it in his name. *Nick Fawcett*

246 Loving God, because we trust you,
we come to you with our concerns.
When illness or injury
causes us disruption, uncertainty,
and the prospect of long-term change;
when we find our lives spinning
out of our control;
give us working knowledge
of your total loving and unchanging presence,
so that in all the changes and troubles of life
we may be assured of your everlasting protection.
Susan Sayers

247 We stand alongside all those who are suffering,
whether in body, mind, or spirit,
and long for your healing and comfort,
your strength for perseverance,
and your patience in the dark times;
we long for your living Spirit to envelop and sustain them.
Susan Sayers

248 Holy God, we bring to you those we know
who are suffering with prolonged illness,
debilitating pain, and emotional distress.
Lay your hands on them to bring relief and healing,
courage to live through this dark time,
and the inner strength which only you can give.
Susan Sayers

249 Lord, in the shock of sudden illness and pain,
and in the tiresome endurance of long-term weakness,
give your peace and tranquility,
your healing and hope. *Susan Sayers*

250 We pray for those who are called to care
for those who are ill in body, mind, or spirit,
that they may bring your healing love and comfort.
Susan Sayers

251 We pray for those who are ill and in pain,
and for those who are sad or frightened.
Surround them with your love and comfort,
and bring them healing.   *Susan Sayers*

252 There are many who hunger for health and wholeness,
freedom from pain or sorrow or doubt.
Feed us, Father, with the Bread of Life.   *Susan Sayers*

253 Lord our God,
we pray for those who have a raw deal in this life;
for those with ongoing health problems,
and all who are caught up in war and deprivation.
We pray for a just and realistic sharing of our resources,
and courage, support, and healing for all who suffer.
Susan Sayers

254 Father, we thank you
for the advances in medical knowledge
and the hope of new treatments for many diseases.
We pray for all in medical research
and all whose lives are crippled or disadvantaged
by illness, frailty, or damage.
Give comfort and reassurance,
healing, wholeness, and peace.   *Susan Sayers*

255 Lord, we pray for all who need medical treatment
or are waiting in pain for surgery.
We pray for those who have become addicted
and long to be set free.
We pray for all whose wrong choices
have ended in heartache, disillusion, and despair.
Susan Sayers

256 We pray for all who are ill at home or in the hospital,
for all in emergency surgery or in casualty;
for those who have just discovered
that they have injuries or illnesses
that will change their lives.
We pray for the work of all who heal and comfort,
all who visit the sick and counsel the distressed. *Susan Sayers*

257 Thank you, Father, for all those who care for the sick,
the unstable, the ungrateful, and the difficult.
We pray for all who are on the receiving end
of hate, deceit, suspicion, or abuse,
and for those who cause others pain
and distress of any kind.
We pray for your healing and transforming. *Susan Sayers*

258 Lord, we bring to you those we know
who are ill or suffering in any way.
Give them healing, restore them
in body, mind, and spirit,
and provide them with your indwelling. *Susan Sayers*

259 Heavenly Father, as we pray for all who are ill
in body, mind, or spirit,
surround them with your love and healing,
your reassurance and peace. *Susan Sayers*

260 We pray for those
who are too weak or exhausted to pray,
but simply know they ache for your comfort. *Susan Sayers*

261 Father, as the sick were brought to Jesus
by their loved ones,
so we bring to you now all those
whom we long to be healed.
May they hear your voice and sense your touch.
Susan Sayers

262 We pray for all who are suffering
through illness, accident, or deliberate cruelty;
for refugees and all who are abused;
that through the caring of human hands
they may experience the caring hands of God. *Susan Sayers*

263 We pray for those who have chronic illness
and have to live in constant pain.
We ask for God's comfort
and reassurance to support them. *Susan Sayers*

264 Father, give courage to those
who have to suffer physical pain
or mental and emotional anguish.
Enable them to draw on your resources
and transform all our pain and sorrow. *Susan Sayers*

265 May all whose bodies cause them pain or immobility
be affirmed in value by loving encounters
with Jesus and his followers;
and may those who are spiritually crippled
be set free to love and serve God. *Susan Sayers*

266 We pray for all suffering from leprosy
and other infectious and life-threatening diseases;
give courage to the long-term and chronically ill
and give respite to those who are at their wits' end.
  Susan Sayers

267 Father, we remember those whose bodies
do not function effectively,
and those whose bodies are abused;
bring some good from their suffering
and healing to their needs. *Susan Sayers*

268 Wherever slow recovery makes time hang heavily,
wherever hope and joy are fading,
we pray for encouragement and delight. *Susan Sayers*

269   We remember those waiting for surgery,
and those in long-term care,
and pray that God's will
may be beautifully accomplished in their lives.   *Susan Sayers*

270   We pray for those in pain
and those whose peaceful lives
have suddenly been shattered.
Help them gather the fragments to start again;
give courage and hope.   *Susan Sayers*

271   Father, we remember those whose bodies ache,
whose spirits shudder,
and whose memories terrify.
We pray for your healing and wholeness.   *Susan Sayers*

272   Father, bring healing and wholeness
to those who suffer, in body, mind, or spirit.
In the sleepless nights and endless days of pain,
give the grace to persevere with patience,
and turn these dark times
into places of spiritual growth.   *Susan Sayers*

273   Healing God, lay your hands on those who suffer,
so that they may know the support of your presence
and find wholeness and peace in your love.
We pray especially for those who are locked
into the conviction
that they are beyond your forgiveness.
May they quickly discover
the freedom of your acceptance.   *Susan Sayers*

274   Wherever there is pain and suffering,
whether physical, emotional, mental, or spiritual,
we pray for your fulsome healing,
and commit ourselves to be available
and ready to help.   *Susan Sayers*

275 Source of Love,
God of Tender Beauty,
Bearer of our Pain,
you accept what we hardly dare name.
You know all,
even more than we can recall.
May we find no part of creation alien.
Embrace in your heart
what we have rejected in ourselves.
Your reflection is in our deepest core.
Flow through
every cranny of our being and our memory
like a pure, life-giving stream,
that we may daily grow more whole. *Ray Simpson*

276 May the strong Lord of life
destroy your disease of body
from the crown of your head to
the base of your heel—
with the power of the Christ of love
and the Creator of the seasons;
with the aid of the Holy Spirit
and the powers of wholeness together. *Ray Simpson*

277 As Christ removed the sleep
from the little child of the grave,
may he remove from you, dear one,
each frown, each envy, each malice. *Ray Simpson*

278 The healing rhythm of the Trinity
I commend you, [name],
in the eye of God,
in the love of Jesus,
in the name of Spirit,
in Trinity of power. *Ray Simpson*

279 *When a person suffers from insecurity or a lack of identity*
An eye was seeing you,
a mouth has named you,
a heart has thought of you,
a mind has desired you:
May Three Persons sanctify you,
May Three Persons help you,
the Father and the Son and the perfect Spirit. *Ray Simpson*

280 *Healing with water*
May this water be for your healing
in the holy name of the Father,
in the holy name of the Son,
in the holy name of the Spirit,
in the holy name of the Three,
everlasting, kindly, wise. *Ray Simpson*

281 Healing Christ,
you walk the world with those who suffer
in broken places of the world.
We come to you with our wounds and theirs.
Encircle those for whom we pray.
Enter their bodies, minds, and spirits.
And heal them of all that harms. *Ray Simpson*

282 All-aware One,
quieten our fevered minds,
subdue our overheated souls,
rest our stressed bodies.
In quietness and confidence be our strength. *Ray Simpson*

283 May the Divine Father
make us instruments of healing.
May the Complete Christ
take from us all that frustrates healing.
May the Holy Spirit
give us power for healing. *Ray Simpson*

284 We invite you, generous Healer,
    into abandoned and wasted areas of our lives.
    Visit these places with compassion.
    Shine kindly and forgiving rays
    of understanding upon them,
    until the beauty that is within us comes forth,
    and our spirits sing again. *Ray Simpson*

285 May we be lit by the glory of God,
    filled with the health of God,
    always tender and true. *Ray Simpson*

286 Great Spirit who broods over the world,
    restore the garment of our self-respect
    and remake us in your beauty.
    Renew in us
    the stillness of our being,
    the soundness of our bodies,
    and bring to dawn our wholeness. *Ray Simpson*

287 Lord, help me to understand my own story,
    to fear nothing except fear itself,
    and to live at peace
    with myself, the creatures, and the world. *Ray Simpson*

288 May failures be forgiven,
    wounds be healed,
    confusions be resolved,
    ignorance be dispelled,
    relationships be treasured. *Ray Simpson*

289 God, Source of our Being,
    we acknowledge that we are fragmented.
    Our communities are suffering.
    Give us courage to look at the wound
    at the heart of everything:
    the wound we run away from,
    the wound we hardly dare name. *Ray Simpson*

290 In each hidden thought our minds start to weave,
be our canvas and our weaver.
In each wounded memory to which we cleave
be our counsel and our healer. *Ray Simpson*

291 We confess that we wound one another.
Our world is disordered.
Accompany us on a journey toward wholeness. *Ray Simpson*

292 Spirit of the living God, present with us now,
circle these we have named.
Enter their bodies, minds, and spirits,
and heal them of all that harms. *Ray Simpson*

293 May illness depart from our eyes.
May weakness depart from our eyes.
May soreness depart from our eyes.
May hardness depart from our eyes.
May sourness depart from our eyes.
May lewdness depart from our eyes,
in the name of the all-seeing Healer. *Ray Simpson*

294 Give us faith that heeds your call to heal.
Give us eyes that see your healing rays.
Give us speech that transmits your healing words.
Give us hands that bring your healing touch.
Give us grace to give to you the glory. *Ray Simpson*

295 Before your Cross, O Christ,
we recollect one story of wounding.
We ask for your mercy
upon this wounded person and people.
We ask your forgiveness for our people.
We ask for the healing of the wound
and the birth of our common humanity. *Ray Simpson*

296   Life-giver, Pain-bearer, Being of Love,
       you hold in your heart our names
       and the hurts we cannot bear to speak of.
       You journey with us through pain
       until you reconcile
       all that we have rejected in ourselves,
       and no part of your creation is alien to us.   *Ray Simpson*

297   We come to God as we are,
       with our hurts and our hungers.
       We come to the One whose love restores us.
       We encircle ourselves and others.
       Heal our ailments.
       Renew our weary frames.
       Make us whole.   *Ray Simpson*

298   Help us, O Healing One,
       to stop dwelling on what others achieve that we don't.
       As we look on the pattern in the palm of each hand,
       we thank you that each is uniquely personal.
       May we grow in confidence, love, and creativity
       according to the designs you have for us.
       We forgive the ones who make us feel inferior.
       Meet their needs; help them find their best course.
       Heal and have mercy on us all.   *Ray Simpson*

299   Forgive our nations for bingeing on borrowed money
       that our children will have to repay.
       Cure our debt addiction.
       Have mercy upon us as we reap what we sow,
       that we may show mercy to one another.   *Ray Simpson*

300   Jesus, when we are weak,
       remind us that your strength
       can reach others through our weakness.
       Open our eyes
       to notice what you notice.
       Open our mouths
       to speak one healing, life-giving word.   *Ray Simpson*

www.ingramcontent.com/pod-product-compliance
Lightning Source LLC
Chambersburg PA
CBHW071219070526
44584CB00019B/3077